THE BOOK OF
STRUMPSHAW

A village at that time of day

STEPHEN PEART

HALSGROVE

First published in Great Britain in 2010

British Library Cataloguing-in-Publication Data
A CIP record for this title is available from the British Library

ISBN 978 0 85704 061 9

HALSGROVE
Halsgrove House,
Ryelands Industrial Estate,
Bagley Road, Wellington, Somerset TA21 9PZ
Tel: 01823 653777   Fax: 01823 216796
email: sales@halsgrove.com

Part of the Halsgrove group of companies
Information on all Halsgrove titles is available at: www.halsgrove.com

Printed and bound by SRP Ltd, Exeter

Title page: Harvest festival at St Peter's c1905.

CONTENTS

Acknowledgements 5

Introduction 7

Chapter 1 **Old Farmyard: new life** 9

The author arrives in Strumpshaw and delves into its history

Chapter 2 **In the beginning there was gravel** 14

Strumpshaw was founded on a hill of minerals left by the Ice Age

Chapter 3 **Lord of the Manor** 19

The title dates from William the Conqueror and remained
evident in 1937

Chapter 4 **Strumpshaw gets its parliament** 21

The parish council is formed in 1894

Chapter 5 **The church of St Peter** 24

The thriving parish church dates from the 13th century

Chapter 6 **The farming community** 40

Once there were six farms but now the farmers live beyond
the village

Chapter 7 **Charity begins at Strumpshaw** 53

The wealthy put something aside for the poor of the parish

Chapter 8 **The mill on the hill** 59

It was one of the most conspicuous landmarks in the county

Chapter 9 **The best days of their lives** 63

Compulsory education brings the school in 1874

Chapter 10 **Goings on in the shed with Helen Hall** 71

Strumpshaw remembers it well-loved characters

Chapter 11 **Blacksmiths, carpenters and wheelwrights** 75

The trades which kept the village in going order

Chapter 12 **Tales of two pubs** 82

The Goat begat the Huntsman and the Shoulder of Mutton
keeps going

Chapter 13   **Strumpshaw Hall: a squire's seat**   90

Stubbe, Springall, Tuck, Gilbert and Holmes: they all came

and went

Chapter 14   **Strumpshaw Fen: a reserved occupation**   99

The RSPB reserve put Strumpshaw on the world map

Chapter 15   **Waiting for trains**   104

Norfolk's first railway is laid through Strumpshaw

Chapter 16   **Think of steam: think of Strumpshaw**   109

Wesley Key puts the village on a different kind of map

Chapter 17   **The wood from the trees**   118

The Domesday survey interprets Strumpshaw as a wooded hill

Chapter 18   **Roads, footpaths and a Long Lane a-winding**   120

Strumpshaw's oldest lines of communication

Chapter 19   **The Post Office**   124

The village's oldest remaining public service

Chapter 20   **All work and a little play**   130

Annual sports day, fetes, films and The Strumpshaw Players.

Chapter 21   **Foreign fields and a certain death**   136

Sixty seven Strumpshaw men go to the First World War

Chapter 22   **A second war and beyond**   142

Fewer men and fewer deaths

Chapter 23   **Round the bend and into Lackford Run**   154

Running water and all things ablutionary

Chapter 24   **Front line Strumpshaw**   159

The village high ground helps England prepare

Chapter 25   **The new generations**   161

People keeping Strumpshaw firmly on the map

Subscribers   167

Acknowledgements

The reward in compiling this book was hearing stories and receiving pictures from people who knew Strumpshaw of old. While some of those folk have passed on, I owe special thanks to the present generations who were willing to recall history of later years.

Participants and contributors who put life into this project were: Kiki Angelrath, Sheila Ashford, Terry & Tony Atkins, Roy Batchelor, Vincent Ball, Chris Basey, Rita & Keith Bedford, Jenny Blackburn, Mike Blackburn, Ted Brighton, Raymond Broom, Rod Brown, Elizabeth Cameron, Jean Childs, Joe Cullum, Daphne Crane, Andrew Evans, Gloria Fagg, Paula Fenton, Barbara Fox, Mary Forder, Iris & Derek Forster, Frank Futter, Dr Martin George, Susan Goodwin, Mary Goward, Hilary Hammond, Steve & Christine Hearnden, Noel Hewitt, Ernest Hoyos, Clive Jermy, Judy Johnston, Rod & Heather Jones, Sheila Ling, Kevin London, Arthur & Rita Marriot, Doris Mayes, Roger Mayor, Christine McNamara, Annie Miller, Mike Page, Anne Payne, Winifred & George Payne, Bruce Rampley, Elsie & Pat Roberts, Paul Rope, Dudley & Pat Rowland, Jim & Jan Saunt, Carroll Sewell, David Stone, Tim Strudwick, John Thrower, Mike Turner, David Varley, Revd David Wakefield, Peter Walker, Lew & Betty Warman and Jenny Williams.

Extra thanks must go to Pat Roberts for acting as scout and go-between.

I am indebted to the editor of The Eastern Daily Press for allowing the use of photographs and quotations from his newspaper's columns which appeared when Strumpshaw was making news.

Thank you to Brundall Local History Group and Barbara & David Pilch for supplying pictures from their respective researches.

Darren Livock, Norwich Supply Manager at Heigham Water Treatment Works, gave information on the main supply.

Final gratitude goes to my wife, Alison, who insisted I contact a publisher and Simon Butler of Halsgrove who answered the call and supported the project.

A sign of the times.

Dedication

John Beck, Harold Broom, Charlie Brown, Barbara Buckton, Alice & Reggie Bunn,
Neville Burton, Joyce Colman, Billy & Edna Cowles, Arthur Grint, Mary & Wesley Key,
Herbert Mayes, Kathy Mills, Fred & Margaret Rope, Hilda Rowland and Clifford Youngs;
whose stories of Strumpshaw life gave rise to this book.

Gloria Fagg's celebrated sketch of St Peter's.

INTRODUCTION

O n Boxing Day morning the 'poor' of Strumpshaw, in Norfolk, gather at the porch of St Peter's church, each to receive a share from four bushels of wheat. This village tradition, unbroken for 250 years, came from the last will and testament of a local farmer, William Black, who died in 1756, decreeing the distribution, should be made from his estate forever.

William Black's benefaction is a most tangible link with the past of this remarkable village. Its geographical fate was fixed during the Ice Age and remains evident to this day through one of the highest viewpoints in the county. At the Domesday survey King William laid claim to his share of Strumpshaw.

For centuries the village survived on agriculture when each ten acres of farmland meant employment for one Strumpshaw labourer and the blacksmith would shoe three horses before breakfast. Now the farmers have gone, yet the fields are fully cropped.

There was a time when the community sustained a dressmaker, undertaker, brick-maker, shoemaker, fish curer and Strumpshaw clay was fired into fine earthenware at Bristol and London. But Strumpshaw life was not always idyllic. People went hungry, children often died at birth and workers on the farms had little soul to call their own.

The church was served with a record incumbency of 57 years by The Revd Edmund Whitbread, a descendant of the celebrated parliamentarian and brewing family. The Lord of the Manor's executors could still collect dues in 1937 and woe betide anyone not in church on Sunday and seated before the squire and his family walked in.

From the threat of Napoleonic invasion to the risk of nuclear attack during the Cold War, Strumpshaw's geographical contours played an integral part in Britain's defence communications.

In present time the village has avoided major development and is home to Strumpshaw Fen, an RSPB reserve of a thousand acres. Two pubs flourish while steam engine enthusiasts flock to its annual rally. The village's landed estate remains in the same family after 130 years and descendants of William Black's family stroll in the community.

In 1981 a group of Strumpshaw folk recounted their lives to me. Whatever their social standing or privations they each recalled how things were done "at that time of day"

Stephen Peart
Strumpshaw 2010

The Mills' family at Oaklands c1910.

Oaklands derelict barn in 1978.

Chapter 1

◇

Old Farmyard: New Life

As the removal van turned into Beech Drive the electricity company's engineer was burying a freshly laid cable, bemused by my family's "skin of the teeth" scheduling. At the rear of the house a painter varnished the last window frame while another chap screeded a concrete path. Beech Drive, Strumpshaw in March 1978 was a building site and we had come to occupy the first of four houses to be completed. The builder's dream was realised; one house sold and occupied would encourage the sale of the others, he hoped.

Beech Drive originally was the stack-yard of the farm once owned by William Black. In 1755 he willed that after his death the 'poor' of Strumpshaw should have an annual share of wheat from the estate, forever. In the 19th century the farm was listed as a large establishment of 200 acres owned by gentleman farmer, Thomas Atkins, giving employment to nine men and one boy. From 1905, Oaklands Farm, as it became known, slithered into a gentle decline with changes of ownership. When its size became less viable the buildings were sold and the fields cultivated by neighbouring farmers. The derelict stack-yard, ripe for development, became a contentious issue in July 1974 when a planning application for ten dwellings was refused. The eventual scheme of fewer houses, complimented with refurbished farm buildings, was deemed right to fit Strumpshaw's planning criteria.

Strumpshaw's rural spread had been sensibly kept free of development. The village acted as a buffer zone separating its two expanding neighbours of Brundall and Lingwood. Strumpshaw was at ease with infilling decaying sites like the old stack-yard. Over the next few months the other properties were built in the drive, the old farm buildings transformed into habitable dwellings and neighbours moved in. Welcoming committees called by and the rector came to tea.

The village comprised of two geographical levels. The lower, always referred to as Low Town with its western border floating eye to eye with the marshes

Suzy and Norby Bothner from Louisiana were amongst the earliest residents in Beech Drive's reconstructed barn.

in the River Yare's valley was served by its thoroughfare of Low Road. There was even a Low Town Farm. The census returns of the 19th century clearly distinguished between "upper" and "lower" Strumpshaw. The census enumerators in the 1800's referred to Upper Strumpshaw as everything beginning at the top of Long lane.

By 1981 little evidence remained to show that Beech Drive had been the garner of a thriving farm. The sites where corn stacks were annually built to await threshing in the winter months were sprouting new lawns and sapling trees. An asphalt road covered the muddy track carved through centuries by farm machinery and livestock. The thatched barn, now commodious accommodation, once echoed to the sound of flails and scrape of winnowing shovels; the tools of threshing by hand. Strumpshaw, like many villages, was gradually eradicating evidence of its past.

The eradication was nothing more sinister than the result of a mechanical revolution. The stack-yard was redundant and where ten acres of Strumpshaw's arable land had once given employment for one labourer, mechanisation brought in the crops.

So what of Strumpshaw's history? For parliamentary purposes the village had been combined with two other parishes, Buckenham and Hassingham, giving a total population of 450. Strumpshaw may have been on the map but hid "lights under its bushels". It supported two public houses, a post office, hosted an annual steam engine rally and was home to a Site of Special Scientific Interest. Depictions of its scenery were preserved for all time by two artists of repute and a descendant of John Sell Cotman once lived in the village. Despite these attributes, persons or bodies had promoted the village's low profile. There were few signposts declaring the village boundaries and two which existed in 1977 were charitable gifts.

Steven Oakley, by the grave of his great great great grandfather, Thomas Oakley, during a visit to Strumpshaw in 2009.

Strumpshaw's history had passed mostly unrecorded so the place to begin retrieval was at the church of St Peter. In the burial ground the village ancestry rested from its labours and the epitaphs spoke clearly; Alexander Goffen, age 78 who died in 1876, was clerk of the parish for 50 years. One of his successors, Thomas Oakley, held the post for 48 years before passing at the age of 73.

Both men were amongst the village elite; in third place after the squire and rector. As scholars, clerks were called upon to witness wills and act as trustees, often combining the job with another trade. In Alexander Goffen's time, the clerk would be called upon to read lessons, sing in the choir, lead the responses, serve at the altar and dig graves if there was no sexton. The position was a function of the church and the candidate had to be:

'...at least 20 years old. Known to the parson as a man of honest conversation and sufficient for his reading, writing and competent skill in singing'

More epitaphs revealed deeper history. Frank Ward, worker on the marshes; John Broom, for thirty-six years a devoted servant at neighbouring Braydeston Hall; Sarah Dingle, Post Mistress; Herbert Mayes, carpenter and undertaker; he had the measure of so many lying in the churchyard. John Spooner, carpenter and publican. Eleanor Thrower, wife of the blacksmith, buried next to Thomas, her infant son, who died at seven months in 1875. Robert, his widowed father took his own life in 1909 and as had been traditional with suicides, would have been buried in the shadow of the church's north side. I could not find his grave.

Thomas Atkins' tomb in Strumpshaw churchyard.

In a family tomb guarded by defensive iron railings laid Thomas Tuck and most of his family. As principal landowner, Tuck tried to stop the laying of the railway through his Strumpshaw estate in 1843. Just a few yards away the marble-topped grave of Thomas Atkins and wife Sarah: he farmed upper Strumpshaw and was happy for a relief line to pass through his fields provided the railway company bridged roadways.

Inside the church were tombs and plaques to the few who definitely lived in uptown. William Springall, Gent. who died aged 65 on 3 November 1757. "He was a sincere Christian who left this life for a better" says his epitaph.

From outside, the sound of earth being dug breaks the morning peace. I discover and meet Harold Broom, for eighty-two years a son of Strumpshaw, working youthfully to level the sunken area of his brother Harry's grave. No stone marks the spot, just a vase and tended grass. The Brooms saw service in the Great War (1914-18), Harold a private in "The Buffs" (The East Kent Regiment) and Harry a gunner in the tank corps. Harold devoted his life and time to St Peter's Church, when he joined the choir at the age of seven; his only absence being for three years war service. Through the stays of eleven rectors he was church warden, sexton, member of the Parish Room Committee and employed by the Barnes family for twelve years. Harold was forthcoming with his life-story lived in the period he constantly called 'that time of day'.

Harold Broom was born in Strumpshaw in 1900. His father was the pork butcher and connected to other village circles , the Ropes, Harrisons and Roses. He talked of farms, growing fields of strawberries and "keeping a few cows". In his day things got done without "argy bargy". When the church path needed new gravel the Barnes organised the work, engaged the manpower and supplied the materials because they owned the village stone pit.

Harold Broom was at home in the churchyard. As sexton he had dug many graves here and seen so many kinfolk committed to the earth. Likewise he had encountered the stratum of Strumpshaw's peculiar clay earth, light in colour and "sticky old stuff". Before Harold's time, it was commercially excavated and sent away to Bristol and London for manufacturing into fine earthenware.

Close to Harold's heart but distant from his brother Harry's grave stands the war memorial. The monument of Cornish granite with its prominent cross displaying the sword of sacrifice bore fifteen leaden names set in a polished face. These were the fellows who never returned after Strumpshaw sent sixty-seven of its proud sons to fight in the 'war to end all wars'. A poster campaign convinced able men that their country needed them for a fight in 1914, which they would win before Christmas. The jingoism and excitement caused some, including Harold Broom, to falsify their ages, to demonstrate manliness and seize the chance to see a world beyond Strumpshaw. Sixty five years on, Harold's memories remained vivid:

'The women who were left had to help on the farms. They took the horses to war as well. Good working people had gone. Somebody would join up so you took the attitude that I shall join up. It went from one to the other. You worked with friends who went; if you're going so am I. I had two brothers; one in the Horse Artillery and one in the Tank Corps'

Harold's mother tried to stop his enlistment but he had convinced the authorities he was a year older than his true 17 years. After the Somme battle of 1916 our country was in need of more men who could be sent to war so Harold was duly accepted.

Until that Great War, men of Strumpshaw had never been sent away to die. Most were born in the village and found work and wives here, if not in the neighbouring parishes. They worked on the farms and ancillary trades and from 1912 at Cantley Sugar Factory, an oasis for employment, across the fields.

On return from the battlefields Strumpshaw was not as Harold remembered it. Like so many men at this time they were unable to take up their former employments in "the land fit for heroes". With the depletion of men to work the farms, a fragmentation had been set in motion and the parish registers show how war changed life in the village. Labourer upon labourer gradually gives way to engineer and factory worker as men sought jobs elsewhere. Experience of the war, seeing fields splattered in flesh and blood, hardened some men to the extent they were no longer afraid to face the privations apportioned by the feudal system.

Harold Broom had been acquainted with my namesake, Russell Peart. Russell became Strumpshaw's blacksmith in 1909 after being set-up at the forge by his father Richard Peart, "the highest paid man at Lingwood station". Brundall born Richard, a platelayer, had helped to lay the railway through the fields of Thomas Atkins. Russell married Strumpshaw girl, Ethel Eagle, a local school teacher. The Pearts were 'chapel people', according to Harold, so they had never figured in Strumpshaw's ecclesiastical circles. Their place of worship was in neighbouring Lingwood where the

Pte Harold Broom, East Kent Regiment, c1916.

Harold Broom as Joseph with Mary, thought to be Phylis Stone appearing in The Nativity at Strumpshaw Rectory c1924.

Harold Broom, 1981.

Methodists had established a meeting place, giving Chapel Road its name in 1867.

People like Harold Broom had little choice for spiritual comfort 'at that time of day'. The local landowners and farmers owned their workers so they had to be seen in church on Sunday and be seated before the squire and his entourage arrived. Harold had accepted it for all his life and although the first war had changed most things, remnants of that past age were evident in Strumpshaw in 1981. The last squire had died more than fifty years ago but there were residents who would stroll into church at the last minute. Even sadder, were others who felt it wrong to sit near the front

Also in that year, most obvious on Strumpshaw's war memorial, was the absence of those who died in the second war. I suggested to Harold the village was lucky in having no losses in the conflict of 1939-45; "but there were a few" he retorted instantly.

How did such an omission remain unnoticed for thirty-six years? Harold could explain it only as "one of those things". The story unfolded into a list of four names, each with family ties in the present day community. How did the local congregation manage to stand around the memorial every year without recognition of what it was acknowledging? Strumpshaw emerged as a place which had not carved its name with pride.

Wedding of Raymond Broom and Madeline Rose, 6 June 1964. Left to right: Harold Broom, Elsie broom, Frank Broom, June Rose, Raymond, Madeline, Stanley Rose, Diane Rose, Hilda Rose, David Rose.

◇

Chapter 2

In the Beginning There Was Gravel

Sometime after the world's creation there came an ice age. England was part of the European continent when a mass of ice slid down from the northern hemisphere bringing all kinds of spoil and materials gathered on its journey. When the bulk of this polar ice covering thawed, the sea level rose and broke the connection with the continent. Around 6,550 years BC Britain was an island and Norfolk's coastline became more or less as we know it today.

For Strumpshaw, the legacy of the ice covering was an eminence, a ridge of hills known to geologists as the Lowestoft Till. This rising ground provided an ideal settlement for the first of the human race, whoever they were, to make camp here.

Some evidence of early human presence in Strumpshaw was discovered in 1954. On 10 April that year workmen were reconstructing flood protection banks on the river Yare and about six feet down, in the peaty clay, they uncovered what appeared to be a human skull. Ted Ellis, then curator of the Department of Natural History at Norwich's Castle Museum was called to make an assessment and recover the find.

The skull was in reasonable condition although its jawbone was missing. Nothing else was found in the

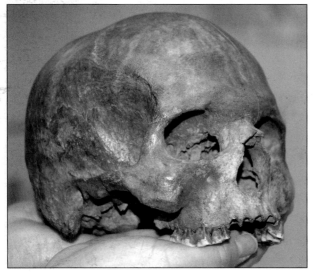

The Strumpshaw Skull at the Castle Museum, Norwich.

vicinity; other bones or fashioned articles which could be associated with the find. Interest mounted because it differed greatly from similar finds in the area. Close examination revealed it possessed characteristics suggesting a relationship with some Mesolithic bones found on the continent, particularly at Teviec in Brittany.

The Mesolithic period was the late time of the stone-age which lasted till 10,000 years before the birth of Christ. Excitement was gradually generated as first opinions were that it was the remains of late Stone age man's presence in this village.

News of the Strumpshaw Skull soon reached students of world anthropology. The find was taken into the care of Dr Calvin Wells (1908-78) a renowned palaeopathologist, resident in Norfolk since the Second World War. He took the skull to France to compare it with specimens from Brittany at the Institute of Human Palaeontology in Paris. His findings were published worldwide in a French journal, "L'ANTHROPOLOGIE" in 1961.

The evidence clearly suggested a male of 30-35 years of age. No other known Mesolithic skull had been found in this region to enable comparison and there was no English example of a post-Mesolithic date to which it might bear any resemblance. It became clear that nobody could affirm that the cranium belonged to the mid Stone Age. But, if it was not precisely Mesolithic the evidence strongly suggested that it was a relatively pure survival of its kind in some more recent era. Sadly, the economics of the time did not permit scientific dating of the find to conclude its identity. Since that time of discovery the skull has remained in the care of the Castle Museum, in Norwich.

Whoever it was who lost his head; whether he lived here or was swept in on some tide, the contours of the land had changed little. The high ground we have today is 130ft above sea level, one of the highest points in the county, known as Strumpshaw Hill. This legacy of the ice age provided the village with a commercial quarry for almost a century as the high ground was a rich deposit of sand and gravel.

At the time of the Enclosure Act an area of just under one acre appears on the maps as 'Surveyors for Gravel'. This small pit was made available for officials to extract mineral materials to keep the local roads in repair. In time, the quarry became known as 'The Poor Hole', giving villager's the right to dig and barrow away sand and gravel for their own purposes. This privilege was jealously guarded into the 1980's by older residents for whom a few kilograms of aggregate was a valuable commodity.

In the twenty-first century The Poor Hole is an attractive conservation area. It remains in the ownership of the village under the auspices of the parish council while its natural state is owed to voluntary service by members of the Blofield and District Conservation Group. Since 1984 their untiring work has led to the ground supporting gorse, broom, blackthorn, dog-rose, foxglove, wood sage and heath groundsel. A small, exposed sandy cliff is the only reminder of the site's history of mineral extraction.

At the centre of Strumpshaw's high ground stood the windmill on its tiny parcel of land. At the enclosures, six acres to the east, in the corner bounded by Buckenham Road and Mill Hill, was in the ownership of Robert Walpole 'for soil' so the quarrying of Strumpshaw Hill was already underway. By the time of the ordnance survey in 1882 there were six gravel pits in operation. Both sides of Mill Hill were being excavated, the field to the east side of Mill Road at the junction of Buckenham Road was yielding sand and stone while digging was underway down Stone Road, where today's recycling site operates.

There was no machinery in the quarry. Men with shovels and sieves plied their back-breaking trade of producing varying grades of aggregates including sand to make bricklaying mortar. Up to ten horses and carts were kept busy carting the stone or sand either on to the roads or across the marshes to Buckenham to be loaded onto wherries for transport to Norwich or Great Yarmouth.

The pit on the opposite side of Mill Hill, where the reservoir stands, was the scene of futile labour in the times of depression. Men were engaged to dig and cart stones and barrow them to the other side of the quarry and tip them out, to justify earning their dole money.

When the quarrying became bigger business the company built houses for its staff. The house on Buckenham's Wood Lane was first occupied by Fred Rudd, a Yorkshireman, who came as foreman to oversee the gravel workings. As the quarry got deeper and the demands for aggregates increased the Strumpshaw gravel pit was yielding all that the ice age had left behind.

In 1916 part of the operation was in the ownership

The Blofield and District Conservation Group clearing The Poor Hole, 2009.

Strumpshaw Gravel pit c1935 with Shepherd Goodwin and Bob Rowland.

Gloria Fagg's sketch of the gravel workings in 1964, showing the Mill House at the top of the hill.

of John Desborough of Mousehold Stone Pits and at the height of quarrying the owner was Edward J Edwards of Plumstead Road, Norwich.

But it could be a dangerous place. Frank Palmer, a 26 year old employee was killed there, on 19 June 1931 when part of the excavation collapsed burying him under 400 tons of gravel and sand. His fellow workers, who escaped injury, immediately set to work in a rescue attempt but it was several hours before they reached Frank's body.

With the second war came an increased demand for sand and gravel. With acres of concrete being laid down in aircraft runways the business became so big that local men jostled the quarry work with the seasonal campaign at Cantley sugar factory. Bob Rowland worked there along with Sunny and Shepherd Goodwin. Bob's son Dudley was 'down there' for three years:

'It was a dangerous place. It was so deep you could have stood Strumpshaw church in there and not be able to see the top above the hole. Big machinery was put in; brought in pieces and assembled in the pit. Once the plant was in they bored a well and dropped a pump in and struck an underground river. When the chap switched it on he said, "It'll run from now to Kingdom Come and it'll never run dry". It was used to wash all the mud away and it all went into a big lagoon'

The days of shovelling and sieving by hand were over but the noise was constant. The sound of gravel being washed and graded carried far on the wind to be heard in every corner of the village. Each change of wind direction meant the clatter was carried to somebody.

Artist and neighbour of the gravel pit from 1960 was Gloria Fagg. To her, the place was a fascination because it was being worked with the constant clank and rattle of the conveyor and lorries to and fro. In the evenings, a walk into the quarry allowed Gloria to absorb the silence and discover wild flowers growing in places where the excavation had been exhausted. But there was forever the sound of loose stones trickling down from the top of the steep sides. By 1961 the quarry had encroached so close to the Poor Hole that the parish council had to enter negotiations with Edward J Edwards for reassurance that the parting grounds would be made good.

When the pit was approaching extinction in 1972 the quarry-men turned their attention to the Poor Hole. Atlas Aggregates, the operators at the time, had encroached on its boundaries as far as permissible and still needed more materials. The company sought permission from the parish council to remove minerals and offered 5 pence per cubic yard with the projected amount being about £600. But after much debate the parish declined the offer and subsequent planning permission to open two more pits was refused, later that year.

The Poor Hole was sought after again in 1976. Another operator, Chic-Grit had need to extract 5000 cubic metres of hoggin for a contract at Cantley Sugar Beet Factory. At any time it is logical to source the materials from a site as near as possible. But again, the parish guarded its mineral deposit even though the price now offered was £1000.

Strumpshaw gravel pit eventually fell silent, that is for the sound of excavations. A totally different intrusion came when the County Council acquired the gaping excavation for use as a landfill site, for domestic refuse, starting in 1976. More aggravation than the quarry had ever generated came in the form of plans for a travellers' encampment, dumping of dead animals and asbestos. Then someone spouted "Radioactive Waste" and everybody was scared. After much investigation, radioactivity to the level of that found on the fluorescent, luminous faces of wrist watches was all that could be measured. For a period of six months there was scaremongering and panic.

Years of filling followed and brought torment for residents nearby. On windswept days refuse lorries would disgorge their loads only to have airworthy content blown against the perimeter fences. Some escaped over the top and often made it half a mile away. There were headlines in the press, letters to councillors and meetings in the parish. In time, the site of some 25 acres was landscaped, only to produce another problem, methane.

Twelve years of compacted and decaying matter was beginning to generate gas. More than one million cubic metres of sand and gravel had been extracted so a lot of decaying matter had filled the space. The walls of the mass excavation were porous

Boreholes are drilled next to the home of Fred Hardesty in October 1985, after methane is found present.

so it was easy for the methane to permeate to the surrounds. As a result, sugar beet was dying in neighbouring farmland and mature oak trees around the site gave up on life. The nearest resident Fred Hardesty was found to have 18% of gas level in his garage and warned not to light a naked flame. Gloria Fagg, next door, smelled gas when digging a hole in the garden to plant a shrub.

But it was not such a shock for the authorities. They had filled big holes before and knew what to expect. It was just that the gas at Strumpshaw had generated quicker than anticipated. In October 1985 equipment was brought in from the former

The methane is flared off in 1986.

Atomic Energy plant at Harwell, boreholes were dug and the gas drawn off and piped to a flaring point. On clear nights the blue flame was a landmark for several miles in all directions.

There were ambitious schemes to use the gas but it carried on burning for 25 years. There was talk of generating electricity on site for connection to the national grid, heating the old folk's bungalows in St Peter's Close or heated glasshouses for horticulture. In this era of green energy it seems incomprehensible that none of the plans ever came to fruition. For

commercial considerations, the gas was not easily compressed and had to be used within two kilometres of the site.

With constant monitoring, a permanent installation sucks the gas out of the waste and burns it at a flare station. Gas monitoring points around the edge of the location show that the system is working and there are boreholes off the site to sample the water for signs of impact by leachate from the waste. The whole place was landscaped with an amenity path laid down for walkers and the site now hides its horrendous past with the help of BADCOG who came along in 2002 and planted 240 shrubs.

But Strumpshaw is not rid totally of that past torment. Out of sight but not out of mind is the recycling centre on Stone Road. It was established as the final vestige of the landfill site where householders from surrounding villages can bring rubbish not taken by the collecting service. Victims of a throwaway society make pilgrimages in cars and often queue to make offerings of glass, paper, wood, garden spoil, metals, cardboard and broken electrical goods. The shuttle of heavy lorries with filled containers and returning empties then have to negotiate roads unsuitable for such traffic.

The landscaped landfill site during its first winter.

Chapter 3

Lord of the Manor

Strumpshaw's last lord was Charles Blackwell Foster, grandson of Sir William Foster, 1st Baronet. He was born in Norwich in 1861, educated at Bury St Edmonds, became a solicitor in 1885, followed by Deputy Coroner for Norfolk; Norwich District, acting Under Sheriff 1891 and a senior partner in Foster, Calvert and Marriott; Norwich solicitors. His family home was Drayton and he also had a house at Lowestoft.

Most of the village's lords never lived in the village. They each acquired the mantel of lordship through historical connections and their general purpose in latter times was to collect arbitrary fines, or taxes, levied against certain tenants under copyhold agreements. In 1908 Charles Foster was dealing with the sale of Brandon House in Hemblington Road through his office, acting as steward for The Manor of Strumpshaw. He died in December 1915

A letter from Charles Blackwell Foster in 1908, Strumpshaw's last Lord of the Manor.

leaving his issue of two daughters, ending a line which had started with the invasion of William the Conqueror in 1066.

The first scribing of Strumpshaw appeared in the Domesday Book. This survey of England was made in 1086 for King William I so that he might have a record of his rights and of the income to which he was entitled from land-tax, rents and any other dues. The book records Strumpshaw as "Stromessaga" among those lands of the king kept by Godric the steward and translates as such:

> 'In Stromessaga two freeman of R(alph) Stalre with sac (the right to hold a court for one's tenants) with eighty-two acres of land, woodland for four swine and then as now, four bordars (villain of the lowest rank, who rendered menial service for a cottage, held at the will of the lord) Then as now one plough between him and the men and in the same (place) another freeman of R(alph) Stalre at the Kings's soke (the right to any fines arising from the court), thirty acres of and eight acres of meadow. Then as now it was worth eight shillings'

The King's manor in 1086 did not extend over the whole of the village of Strumpshaw, for part belonged to the great manor of Willam de Beaufoe, Bishop of Thetford, who bequeathed it to the See of Norwich. In the year 1095 Bishop Herbert of Losinga, the first bishop of Norwich, granted it to his steward, Guy, who took his surname from the village of Braydeston.

Early in the 12th Century, King Henry 1 gave the manor of Strumpshaw to a certain Odo de Danmartin. It remained in his family until the middle of the next century, when the male line came to an end and the manor was divided among the heiresses. Part went to Sir John de Botetourt, a prominent baron who had married Maud de Danmartin and part to a Stephen de Strumpsawe (Strumpshaw) who is said to have sold it to William, the fifth Lord Bardolf, and Juliana his wife. Little is known of this episode but it is quite clear that by 1300 the whole manor was owned by a family called Bardolf and it remained in their hands until the middle of the 15th century, when they also died out. Their supposed powerful line was broken.

T Hugh Bryant, who wrote extensively on Norfolk churches in 1908, delved into Strumpshaw's surviving manorial notes and published his findings in the *Norwich Mercury*:

> 'This lordship passed to the Beaumonts and to Sir William Arundel, Lord Matravers and Anne his wife in 1347. In 1554, Henry, Earl of Arundel, conveyed it to Queen Mary and she granted it to Sir Nicholas Hare. In 1562 Robert Hare Esq was lord of this manor and Clerk of the Pells and died without issue. Sir Ralph Hare aliened it, in 1607, to Sir Thomas Berney of Reedham, in which family it afterwards remained, until it was sold, with Reedham, to Sir James Edwards and afterwards to Sir Lambert Blackwell and so to the Leathes family. It subsequently passed to Reginald Henry Neville, Esq, who died in 1878, having married Lady Dorothy Walpole, a sister of the Earl of Orford. The two manors of Braydeston and Strumpshaw were offered for sale in 1896, in Norwich, but failed to find a purchaser. The present (1908) Lord of the Manor is R H C Neville, Esq of Wellingore, Lincolnshire'

R H C Neville held the manor until 1912 before it came into the hands of Charles Blackwell Foster. After his death the holding was in the hands of his trustees, remaining so in 1937.

Homeward bound from Low Road, July 2009.

Chapter 4

Strumpshaw gets its Parliament

Until 1894 there was no level of Parliament within reach of Strumpshaw's people. The Local Government Act which came into force that year enabled parochial control of social welfare and duties in the village. Hitherto, these had been the domain of a variety of groups based around the church. Above parish level, Strumpshaw was one of nineteen villages in the Blofield Union which since 1834 had replaced the Blofield Hundred. A Hundred was a subdivision of the county; Norfolk consisted of thirty three, and they were listed from the time of the Domesday Book in 1086. The hundreds were units of administration and taxation dating from a system of government in the 8th century. The feudal system would not disappear overnight and there were those who would hang on to manorial rights to the end.

The Local Government Act of 1894 was the result of reforms passed through Parliament and reached our level after much debate and opposition. The act's first requirement was that a parish should convene an annual meeting on 25 March or within seven days either side of that date and if necessary elect a parish council. The process was not as simple as we know life today: only certain people in the village had the right to vote, for anything.

Strumpshaw's inaugural meeting of electors took place on 4 December 1894 at 7-30pm. While the minutes did not record the place, the records detailed everything by the book. The rector, Rev A J Barton was nominated chairman by Robert Thrower, the blacksmith and seconded by Edward Barnes, one of the village's chief landowners. Then followed a list of those nominated for councillors: Thomas Atkins, farmer; Rev A J Barton (withdrew); Henry Flowers, a corresponding secretary; William Harrison, junr, shopkeeper; William J O Holmes, Strumpshaw Hall; John Howes, labourer; William Oakley (withdrew), Edward Pike, Miss Frances Pike; William Ramm, platelayer; Stephen Rope, gardener and Robert Rose, platelayer. The withdrawals reduced the list to nine candidates and a show of hands produced the seven councillors, as required by law. Henry Flowers,

William Harrison, John Howes, Edward Pike, William Ramm, Stephen Rope and Robert Rose were elected the first Strumpshaw Parish Council. Their election expenses had amounted to £1.5s.4d (£1.27p) but the sum was not announced until a special meeting, one year later.

The first meeting of the councillors was held at 7pm on 13 December 1894, at the home of Henry Flowers, in Low Town, because a room in the school was not available. Rev Barton came along to chair the gathering but after a show of hands Henry Flowers was elected chairman. After all, it was his house! He was the Corresponding Secretary, Norwich District, Manchester Unity of Oddfellows. Thomas Atkins was also present to give information to the new council in his capacity of parish overseer. The business of finding a clerk was put off until the next meeting. Putting things off until the next meeting was the parish council's forte, at that time.

The wait was short. The next meeting was convened at the school, on 20 December. Nobody elected wanted the job of clerk but somebody knew a man who was willing, Mr B N Menison of Brundall. After proposal and seconding he was engaged at the salary of £4 a year along with Geoffrey Fowell Buxton Esq a member of Gurney & Co, bankers, of Norwich who consented to be treasurer. Strumpshaw Parish Council was in business.

From that time on, the council took responsibility for any affair deemed in the village interest. One year later the members wanted to know the state of parish charities and took the offer of Rev Barton to talk them through the Enclosure Award of 1822. A highlight of the award was the Poor Allotment, consisting of ten acres two roods of marsh, the rents from which bought fuel for the needy of Strumpshaw. The Lord of the Manor, the Rector, Churchwardens and Overseers were its trustees. Strumpshaw's lord at that time was Charles Blackwell Foster (1861-1915), a senior partner with Norwich solicitor Foster Calvert and Marriott.

New trustees in place of the churchwardens and

Parish Meeting. Dec 4 1894.

The first Meeting of Electors under the Parish Councils Act was held at 7.30 p.m. on Dec 4th 1894. The Revd. A. J. Barton was nominated Chairman by Mr R. Thrower and seconded by by Mr. Edward Barnes. No other gentleman being proposed Mr Barton took the Chair. The names nominated for Councillors were Mr. J. Atkins; Revd. A. J. Barton (withdrew); Mr Henry Flowers; Mr Wm Harrison, Junior; Mr W.J. Holmes (withdrew) Mr J Howes; Mr Wm Oakley (withdrew) Mr. Edward Pike; Miss Frances Pike; William Ramm; Stephen Rope; and Robert Rose.

After the withdrawals there were 9 candidates left on the list — On a show of hands the following were duly elected Parish Councillors. Henry Flowers; Wm Harrison, Junior; John Howes; Edward Pike; William Ramm; Stephen Rope; & Robert Rose. The meeting closed at 8.30 p.m. A unanimous vote of thanks was accorded to the Chairman propos. Mr W.J. Holmes. Secd. Mr Edward Barnes.

A. J. Barton
Chairman.

December 4th 1894.

Strumpshaw.

Names of Council Elected at first Parish Meeting

Henry Zachariah Thompson Flowers
William Harrison (Junior)
John Howes
Edward Pike
William Ramm
Stephen Rope
Robert Rose.

Minutes of Strumpshaw's inaugural Parish Council meeting, December 1894.

overseers were appointed. These were; Edward Barnes, William J Holmes, William Ramm and Stephen Rope. Then it was the turn of the William Black Corn Charity to get new trustees. Mostly the same names were elected; Edward Barnes, William J Holmes, Edward Pike and Stephen Rope. The parish council was making its presence felt and the Charity Commissioners acknowledged the candidates. In the following January the council was able to report that 228 one hundred weight sacks of coal had been delivered to the poor of the parish.

In April 1895 the council had to meet at The Shoulder of Mutton as the school was in use by the pupils for an evening entertainment. This opened with discussion on the terms of using the school for meetings. The School Board wanted three shillings (15p) per meeting which included light, firing and cleaning the school after use. The council understood that the act of Parliament allowed it to use the school to meet, free of charge, but wrote to the board suggesting the charge of three shillings for the facilities was excessive. The board met to consider and made a reduction to two shillings and sixpence per meeting, in translation that amounts to twelve and a half pence in today's money.

The pattern of council business through the years changed very little. Councillors were replaced as members left the parish or others came along for nomination. Issues of road conditions were forever raised, school managers appointed and requests for allotments had to be dealt with. At one point, seven parishioners were asking for a total of 22 acres. A milestone moment came on 14 January 1916 when the council met in the new parish room for the first time. The room was built in 1915 as a gift to the parish by the daughters of Edward Barnes who had served as trustee to village charities.

By the outbreak of the First World War the council had to deal with matters of National Service, Norfolk War Agricultural Sub Committee and War Saving Certificates but very little was reported or acted upon. In 1925 the district council objected to new council housing, at the bottom of Long lane, being called Council Cottages so it was agreed to rename them South View Cottages.

Years of parish housekeeping occupied the meetings until another milestone, the appointment of Strumpshaw's first female councillor, Catherine Jane Barnes, on 10 March 1931.

With her sisters she had donated the land and money to build the Parish Room. The new council also included Harold Broom, an employee of the Barnes family, first war veteran, sexton, churchwarden and a member of the parish room's founding committee.

Much of the parish councils business over the years was perennial. A very delicate item often on the agenda was the Parish Pit and its adjoining allotment, a small parcel of land in the corner at the junction of Barn Hill and Buckenham Road. Confusion often arose in relating it to the Poor Hole, further up the road. The Parish Pit was always a watering hole, to take surface draining and together with its neighbouring, allotted ground, totalled about a seventh of an acre. At the time of the Enclosures it was assigned to the Surveyor of Highways. As recent as 1963 the Rural District Council conceded the land, after its ownership came into question, was vested in the interest of the Parish Council.

The dawn of each new age challenged Strumpshaw Parish council, as far as politics affected the village. The issues became more serious and varied with an increase in dealing with planning applications as the council was given the first look to comment on proposed developments. The names of councillors changed every four years and more frequently, the seats were filled by newcomers to the village.

Strumpshaw's stalwart parish councillor during the second half of the twentieth century was Sheila Ashford. Her position filled a casual vacancy in January 1959, under the chairmanship of 'Buster' Bracey and opened the way for an illustrious calling into local politics. Sheila accepted parish council chairmanship in May 1962 and willingly held the position until 1983. Running parallel, and far beyond her local council position, Sheila took nine years as a Strumpshaw School Board Manager, a spell of teaching, a district councillor, nine years as a magistrate, Chairman of Blofield Deanery Synod for 19 years and membership of various committees in the region.

Parish councillors have often been easy targets for critics who most of the time outnumber willing participants, one hundred fold. The task is thankless and by law it has to be performed by somebody. Whatever the arguments, for or against, Strumpshaw Parish Council, for more than one hundred years, has maintained the village on its preferred course.

Jimmy Key, Wesley Key and Sheila Ashford, Boxing Day 1983.

Chapter 5

The Church of St Peter

On 9 July 2009 the Revd David Wakefield was instituted and inducted as the Rector of South Burlingham, Lingwood and Strumpshaw with Hassingham and Buckenham. The institution in St Peter's Church Strumpshaw, by Bishop David of Thetford, elevated Revd Wakefield to Rector, from Priest in Charge, his position since filling the vacant post in 2007. His institution provided security for the group of parishes who proved they could work together; adding David Wakefield to an illustrious

Bishop David of Thetford and Revd David Wakefield.

list of Strumpshaw's incumbents, recorded from 1258.

There is no mention of a Strumpshaw church in the Domesday Book. When the survey was made in 1086, King William's manor did not extend over the whole of this village because part of it belonged to William Beaufoe, Bishop of Thetford. In due course, he bequeathed it to the See of Norwich. The church had obviously been built on the bishop's territory and appears in the Taxation of Norwich, a valuation of the county's churches in 1254.

History shows the village was always prosperous. When a visitation of the parishes was ordered by the Archbishop in 1603 Strumpshaw was valued at £8, with its adult population of fifty two souls. From 1727 the same rector served Strumpshaw and Braydeston. In 1792, Strumpshaw with its population of 412 and Braydeston with 126, were consolidated into one benefice with a value of £50.

Many years on, in 1949, the Church Commissioners changed the living. A scheme, by which the three benefices of Strumpshaw and Braydeston; Buckenham and Hassingham; and Witton with Brundall, became two. The new order received Royal Assent in March 1951 and the historic connection of Strumpshaw with Braydeston was severed.

In architectural terminology St Peter's church Strumpshaw is a long building of flint in the Early English (13th Cent) and Perpendicular styles. The latter style appeared two hundred years on whereby the walls consisted mainly of windows leaving enough support for the roof. Then with various changes and restorations in Victorian times, culminating in a vast re-roofing operation in 2006, the church we see today is the result of ongoing modification and repair

While the church was constructed in different stages the tower was added last. Katherine Gilbert of North Burlingham, in her will dated 1489, left a coomb of malt to enable a steeple to be added to St Peter's. The lofty tower with pinnacles and stepped battlements contains three bells.

Strumpshaw church, c1890.

Paul Ashford, churchwarden and Revd George Humphreys during repairs to the parapet c1963.

Above: *The Whitbread crest on bench ends in St Peter's.*

Left: *The double piscina in St Peter's.*

Two separate steeply-pitched roofs of thatch had covered the continuous nave and chancel until 1818. Thatched roofs were of a steeper pitch to cast off the rainwater. Deterioration was evident early in the 19th century by the amount of times the churchwarden's accounts record the need for repairs. The solution in 1818 was to replace the roof with slate, including some timbers, at a cost of just under £150.

With the removal of the thatched roof the nave walls were also lowered to the height of those of the chancel. The shallower pitch of the replacement, slated roof gave the tower a lofty appearance earning a comment from Nicholas Pevsner in his book, Churches of Norfolk, that the church had a "curiously rigid appearance"

St Peter's Strumpshaw caters for the architecturally excitable. A painted 15th century rood screen separates nave from chancel. On the south wall of the sanctuary is a fine Early English double piscina with moulded arches. These ecclesiastical washing-up bowls are where the priest would cleanse his fingers before consecration and rinse the chalice at the close of the service. On the same side, further along the wall is a sedilla. Like three steps, these were seats for the priest and his two assistants, for their use at times during Mass.

From 1834 Strumpshaw's rector was the Rev Edmund Salter Whitbread. His grandfather was Ive

Whitbread, whose half-brother Samuel started the successful Whitbread Brewery in 1742. The Rev Whitbread's incumbency lasted for 57 years until his death at the age of 87 in 1890. During that time at St Peter's he baptised 577 children and officiated at 108 marriages and 406 burials. The church benefited from his wealth as he paid for much of the upkeep during his incumbency.

The chancel was restored and re-seated by Revd Whitbread in 1848. He paid for stained glass in four Early English windows and the Perpendicular east window. The poppy-head pews in the chancel were also given by him with his family's arms and crests carved on the ends.

Edmund Salter Whitbread married Charlotte Josselyn of Sproughton in Suffolk. They raised five children in Strumpshaw; Charlotte 1832-90, Edmund 1836-68, Emma 1838-1919 William 1844-1925 and Frederick 1848-1922. A family tragedy was the early death of eldest son Edmund; killed in New Zealand after serving as a captain in the Maori Wars. He is buried in Wanganui and commemorated by a memorial here, in the sanctuary.

At his passing in November 1890 Rev Whitbread was remembered as a kindly and genial character. He was the oldest clergyman in the Blofield district and the oldest magistrate on the Blofield bench, where he served for twenty five years.

Rev Whitbread's successor was Revd A J Barton. He undertook restoration at his own expense in 1893 involving almost the whole building. He replaced the old box pews with open benches to hold a congregation of 160. A new organ came the following year followed by renewed chancel windows and a new pulpit in carved oak. During the course of all this overhauling, a long upright narrow recess was uncovered in the north wall of the nave, just by the splay of the door. Some authorities were content this had been a locker for holding a processional cross or banners. The opening was found filled with rubbish, amongst which was a block of dark Purbeck marble with two shallow pointed arches. It may have formed part of an earlier font but nobody really knows.

Revd Alfred Barton's restoration works could be taken as his own memorial. Within living memories he was a notable incumbent but was quite a disciplinarian as Harold Broom recounted:

'He wouldn't allow any idle chatting in church, after the service. "If you've got any business to talk about then please go outside" he'd say. We had a full choir, about thirty at that time. He was very particular about the surplices. They all had to be starched. If it was the time of chestnut picking he would have a look at our hands before we robed up to make sure they were clean. He was like the squire; you had to touch your hat to him if you saw him coming down the road. He had sway in the village but of course if anyone was ill in the parish they would look for the rector to come and visit'

The question often arose as to how incumbents were able to pay to keep God's house in order, out of their own pockets. Some dependency was on the patrons of the benefice, the landed gentry on whose ground the church had been built. Then there were the tithes and the rector's Glebe Land. In olden times, farmers in the village had to pay one tenth of their income to the church.

Farmers were not forever keen on paying one tenth, so in 1844 the tithes were commuted, and paid as fixed rent. At Braydeston in 1892, for instance, the gross yearly value was £490, a very large sum at that time of day. As for the Glebe Land, Strumpshaw's sixty four acres in 1892 included Church Farm opposite St Peter's. This provided an income for the rector through being let to local farmers.

Revd Thomas Butcher was rector here until 1933. He is best remembered for a magnificent pageant presented in the grounds of the Rectory in July 1932. Revd Butcher was associated with missionary work in Melanesia, a group of islands in the Pacific, north and north east of Australia. His associate, Bishop John Steward of Melanesia, narrated a performance in the gardens to portray missionary work in the

The Melanesia pageant in the rectory gardens, 1932. Left to right, back row: Lenny Stevens, Gordon Brown, Dick Atkins. Lewis Grint, Fred Stevens. Front: Rex Davies, Donald Brown, Fuller Pilch, Arthur Grint.

Pacific islands. The rector, parishioners and boys and girls of the choir all played parts. There were few props; the lawn was the stage with the trees and bushes making a realistic backdrop.

After years of weathering St Peter's roof showed signs of dilapidation again. In 1957 the old slates were replaced but not in the best manner. All kinds of timbers had gone into the roof structure at various times to keep the work economical. Inside, a ceiling of hardboard, painted blue, hid the irregular timberwork with its severe woodworm infestation. The ceiling was a most incongruous addition given the medieval importance of the building.

In due course Strumpshaw's Glebe lands were disposed of by the Diocese. In the name of economies the rectory was sold, along with much of its grounds as building plots for housing development. The last full time rector, occupying the old rectory, had been Charles Coleman and he is remembered for being surrounded by eight acres of nettles and his fascination for Strumpshaw's blacksmith. A small modern counterpart rectory, the first bungalow style in the diocese, was built and made ready for a new incumbent.

If a medal had been struck for Strumpshaw's favourite rector it would have gone to George Hall. He was installed in 1966 and made long lasting impressions from the start. He is often recalled for three things; the renovation of the church bells, organising French Fairs and "going to the Shoulder of Mutton for a fag and a pint"

In August 1969 Revd Hall introduced the village to an experience of France. There was a Great Snail Race, French wines were tasted, cheeses were

Left, Bishop Lancelot Fleming with Revd George Hall, 1968.

Poster for the French Fair.

Cicely Fancy giving voice to the bells in 2009.

The church bells about to leave for Loughborough bell foundry in February 1968. Left to right, back row: Lorry driver, Harold Broom, Revd George Hall, Grace Atkins, Mrs Cunningham, Mrs Rose. Front, on lorry: Annie Hooker, Joyce Colman. (PICTURE BY COURTESY OF EASTERN DAILY PRESS).

sampled and the latest French cars were tested, all in a gay (not today's parlance!) Parisian atmosphere, along with the aroma of garlic bread. A local baker competed to bake the longest French stick in the world and it reached 39 feet! The event attracted 3000 visitors and the villagers had known nothing like it. It was a just reward for the fete's eighteen months of planning.

The event brought one amusing incident. Henry Barrie, a total newcomer arrived in the village the day of the first fair having moved from London with his work. He was stunned and surprised to be confronted in Norwich Road by a Gendarme and for a moment seriously questioned the nature of the place he had chosen to live. He had met Harold Broom masquerading for George Hall's French Fair! Such was the success of the event, that others followed.

Harold Broom as a Gendarme for the French Fair, with Betty Warman.

When the Revd Hall took office the three bells at St Peter's had been silent since 1960. Undisturbed since 1620 they were pronounced unsafe when their supporting headstock and framework was found to be ravaged by death watch beetle. For safety, the bells were removed from the belfry in 1966 and stored at ground level. George Hall had been resident just three months and had to deal with the task. £500 was required for a renovation programme at John Taylor's, the bell founders of Loughborough.

Revd Hall was worried that the money ought to be spent in other ways as there was much needed abroad. But the church was the centre of faith in the village so the bells were given priority. The fund started with £200 from private subscriptions followed by local functions. There was a sponsored walk by teenagers of the Pathfinders Organisation, a Festival of Flowers at Easter and a Garden Party.

After refurbishment the bells were hung "dead" and rung by pulling ropes to strike the clappers. On 23 June 1968 the bells were heard to peal over the village once more, after a special confirmation service and dedication by the Bishop of Norwich.

The three bells had summoned parishioners to worship, celebrated weddings and tolled mournfully at internments for well over 400 years. By comparison, the organ was very young. The current instrument, built by Norman Beard of Norwich in 1893, was reinstalled after refurbishment in about 1909. Betty Warman, the resident organist for around fifty years could trace her family's association with the

church's music for more than a hundred years.

Betty, then Betty Rose, started piano lessons at the age of eight. By the time she was competent her mother was teaching at Sunday School and got her to play the hymns. More practice and lessons in Norwich led to her filling in with Mrs Knights who played at Strumpshaw and Braydeston. In the early days, before electricity, her mother pumped the organ to generate the air. It could be tiring work, keeping the lead weight indicator above a certain line to show there was sufficient air to fill the pipes. Other pumpers who came along were Gerald Fox and David Soanes. Young Gerald pumped away to raise the wind then read his comic until the music suddenly wilted, causing him to resume pumping!

In the wakes of comings and goings of rectors there was some sadness. Few occasions were more wrenching than the levelling of the babies' graves in the churchyard. Either side of the path between the kissing gate and the tower, were buried the village infants of tragic passings: some christened, others not, while many were still-born. Some had been buried at dead of night, by grieving parents so desperate to place their infants in consecrated ground after an official burial had been refused.

Betty Warman, 2009.

1958 Nativity in St Peter's, Strumpshaw. Left to right, back row: ?, ?, ?, ?, Evelyn Knights, Dorothy Wooler, Pat Roberts, Carrol Piggin, ?, ?. Front: Mary Nurse, Harold Broom.

Arthur Grint's mother and sister.

Pat Roberts by the plots of the flattened babies' graves.

Little Frank Rowland is somewhere there with Iris Grint the young sister of Arthur. She died soon after they had moved from Lingwood to Strumpshaw. Iris Forster's aunt Mabel lost a baby boy and he lays there, somewhere. Iris remembers her aunt cycling over to visit Hill Rise from Blofield and tending the little chap's grave.

In 1929 Cecil and Lily Curtis lost their third child John at just four days. His grave is unmarked, somewhere by the path on the Buckenham Road side of the churchyard. Most poignant was Patricia Mary, born at home, in The Loke, to Elsie and Ronald Roberts. She lived for a mere five minutes and was baptised by Dr McKelvie who had just delivered her. She was buried on the 19 June 1945. Her short life is more than a memory for her sister, who took the name of Patricia, and fondly recalls tending the grave of her elder sibling.

It was during the time when drastic measures were needed to keep the churchyard tidy. The generally accepted scheme was to lose mounds and kerb stones to enable free passage of mowing machinery. The babies' burial spots had been mounds without stones yet many had been regularly attended.

Revd George Hall moved on and from Northampton came Revd Albert Bransby. He combined a seven year ministry here with his position of hospital chaplain from 4 April 1975 until retiring in August 1982. There followed a period under

the cover of Brundall until the next Priest in charge and the benefice's first woman incumbent, Revd Vivien Elphick from October 1994 to 2006.

Early in 1990 the roof slates were seen to be coming apart. Re-fixing was necessary following any high wind and a hole in the south elevation was letting water into the building near the font. Fortunately for St Peter's, one of the churchwardens, David Varley, understood buildings, passionately.

The plight of the church was noted at the quinquennial of 1995. When this five yearly inspection was due, David Varley assisted the ecclesiastical architect's survey of the fabric by photographing what was lurking above the false ceiling of painted hardboard. A small aperture at the end of the covering allowed no more than a peep-show of the rot and dilapidation lying within, brought on by beetle attack. With the aid of a camera and floodlighting, David Varley produced a gallery of pictures but not all of the Parochial Church Council (PCC) members were convinced.

To untrained eyes, David's pictures showed an old building but he knew the roof was close to collapsing about holy ears. Confirmation from the specialists forced the PCC into action as some members needed convincing. By the end of 1995 the PCC agreed to proceed with a scheme to replace the roof and invited three architects to submit their ideas. Two designs were then presented and early in 1998 the accepted plan had been submitted by Purcell Miller Tritton.

The PCC faced its task of raising the estimated cost of £100,000. A gift day in June 2002 raised an extraordinary £30,000 followed by a round of fundraising

Revd Albert Bransby with Andrew and Roslyn Evans, 30 October 1976.

Revd Vivien Elphick at The Old Rectory garden party.

David Varley, passionately caring for St Peter's.

The first art exhibition in 2003.

activities while sponsorship was sought for tiles and roof trusses. But the projected cost soon elevated to £140,000. Forty one trusts were approached, yielding £18,000 but the bulk depended on the parishioners and their fund-raising activities.

A committee was formed and launched the "Keep it Covered" appeal. All manner of events were organised: concerts, barbecues and art exhibitions while local celebrities pledged support. Alan Gray, gardener and writer; Richard Hughes, chef and restaurateur and Keith Skipper, press columnist, all came to the aid of St Peter.

By 2006 there was enough money to start work. Under the discerning eye of church architect, Nigel Sunter, scaffolding appeared round the church in May. In the meantime, church services were held in the parish room. When the workmen set about removing the roof, eight inch square beams simply broke in two. David Varley's worst fears had been totally justified. The archaeological surveyors came in, another requirement of such schemes, and deduced that the roof had been constructed of secondhand timbers in the 19th century. The mouldings present on the second-hand trusses suggested an ecclesiastical source.

When the new roof was completed early in 2007 the western arch could be seen from inside the church for the first time in 200 years. While the design reflects the scale and form of its medieval predecessors it is set firmly in the 21st century. Laminated, wooden arched beams and purlins with steel tie rods and connectors were skilfully applied. The external covering with clay pantiles caused a few parochial shocks but the colour was promised to darken with age. All settled well in time for a service of dedication, 17 March 2007.

A final embellishment was added in April 2009. The triangular gap left where old and new roofs joined was filled with a modern stained glass window. It depicted a journey of life, with bright colours symbolising childhood and ranging darker shades to capture old age. It was the work of Karim Yasamee, a Norwich-based artist, commissioned by Nick and Judy Price of Strumpshaw as a memorial to their respective parents.

In July 2009 when the Bishop of Thetford installed Rev David Wakefield as rector in the combined benefice it represented, for him, a welcome and secure future in Strumpshaw. The list of previous incumbents, on record from the year 1257, had for

St Peter's prepared for re-roofing.

The old roof removed.

The churchyard becomes a building site.

The new roof and lighting, 2009.

Karim Yasamee prepares to insert the new stained-glass window, 2009.

Revd David Wakefield and Heather entertain at the children's garden party, 2009.

David Wakefield with his parents and sisters at the time of his christening.

Joan and Michael Powlesland at the garden party, 2009.

Right: Sheila Ashford at the rectory garden party 2009.

...been uninterrupted. David's arrival
...t chapter of St Peter's history:

...ast is another country; they do
... . And if I look back at my own
...ething of the major changes
...ral ministry in my own life-
... worse.

...1964. My mother Hilda,
...dwife with her; but not
...g service. He wasn't
...g seen it all before (I
...d Doreen). It was
...had charge of his
... son was not a
...ay I think that's differ-
..., certainly for women priests,
...ve wouldn't it? But even the men
...pected to have a family life outside of church
...a way that I don't think it was expected then.

Not that I would complain at all about my child-
hood. We lived in a huge 18th century Vicarage in
Walton, Felixstowe. I can see that for my parents it
was a challenge to maintain on a minister's stipend
(salary), but to me it was a place of adventure. I sailed
my toy boat when the water table rose in the cellar but
there were drawbacks. I had to run the long distance
from the bedroom to the bathroom as we couldn't heat

the whole house, and there was ice on the inside of the
windows. My bedroom was so large, that although an
adventure for a young boy, I developed a habit of
leaving things where I had used them. A habit my
wife still hasn't quite broken and she finds less than
helpful, in a smaller (though still spacious) modern
Rectory. She though, isn't sure she would swap it for
an old style Rectory. Whilst we truly appreciate
Elizabeth Cameron generously sharing the wonderful
Old Rectory and its grounds in Strumpshaw with the
community, the purpose built Rectory in Lingwood is
much easier to heat and clean.

It's not only the demise of many of the old Rectories
that have changed in rural ministry. When my father
was first ordained in 1951, it was quite common to be
placed in charge of one parish. Now rural communi-
ties are mostly grouped together in benefices. I am
fortunate that I have South Burling-
ham, Lingwood, Strumpshaw, Hassingham and
Buckenham. Some vicars are already being asked to
pastor 13 or more parishes. But even with 5 this
means the way of ministry changes. Whilst the priest
still retains a pastoral and teaching role, he or she
must become a facilitator discerning, encouraging,
enabling and supporting the lay people in the commu-
nities to help their churches grow. In a sense perhaps
this is not altogether new.

St. Peter talks in 1 Peter 2 of the priesthood of all

Elizabeth Cameron at the garden party, 2009.

Rupert and Jo Crisp, garden party 2009.

Strumpshaw Church Choir c1980. The photograph includes: Roger Breame, Iris Gale, Julie Foley Wyatt, Joyce Colman, Joan Powlesland, Andrew and Ros Evans, Marie Breame, Betty Warman, Terry Dabbs, Henry Barrie.

believers. We need to recognise that the modern minister cannot do it all him or herself. I am fortunate in Strumpshaw to have excellent Churchwardens, PCC members, Readers, a lay worship leader and others willing to share in the ministry in this place and to work within the benefice to build up the church.

God gifts us all to contribute to his work in different ways. I left school when I was 17 with no thought of following my father into the ministry. I worked for many years happily for Rank Hovis in their flour mill at Felixstowe Dock, and travelling around the country to different mills as IT projects required. I first met Heather at church, but before we married in 1996 I assured her that I had no intention of giving up what was a largely comfortable and interesting life, to become a vicar. I was happy contributing to church life by leading what used to be called Sunday School. That changed around the turn of the millennium when I began to hear God's call to

be an ordained minister. I initially tried to avoid it as I didn't think I was cut out for the role. Perhaps with the style of ministry in the past, that may have been true. But as I explored the question I found that ministry had changed. Ministers in many rural settings now need to be much more members of a team than used to be the case. Those who select and train priests assured me that they did see a place for me as a priest in the Church of England. And now I find that place here in this benefice among others gifted in different ways to work together as church to serve the community.

In November 2009 Strumpshaw's PCC was commended for its work in the community. The Campaign to Protect Rural England, Norfolk awards considered the new nave roof of St Peter's and its lighting scheme worthy of recognition. The judges chose Strumpshaw's project as an example of how a community is keeping the county alive.

David Varley and the CPRE award, December 2009.

Chapter 6

◇

A Farming Community

Once upon a medieval time the fields around Strumpshaw were not as we see them today. Much of the village's 1337 acres of arable land and marshes was open common ground, worked by its people and grazed by their animals. The few landowners were freemen who had been awarded property in return for supporting the Lords. Serf's worked their Lord's land and in due course, paid rent and gradually built farms of their own. They became yeoman, or freeholders, the link between gentry and labourers.

Towards the end of the 19th century Strumpshaw's land was subjected to the Enclosure Act. This new law abolished the open-field system of farming with locals claiming their appropriate piece of land before fences divided the plots. A look at Strumpshaw's enclosure maps show a mosaic of small parcels of land attributed to various individuals. The new act was meant to improve farming methods and productivity.

One of the large freeholders in the village at this time was William Black. He died in 1756, without issue, so the farm, known as Oaklands for much of the 19th and 20th centuries, passed to his nephew, Thomas Atkins. The farm was handed successively from father to son, Thomas Atkins, for one hundred and fifty years as the first son of each generation was named Thomas. The family witnessed good times; waited on by servants while one daughter married William Redhead, a London gentleman.

Thomas Atkins' (1849-1920) name appeared on numerous wills as a respected witness. He sat on the board of guardians for the Blofield District but in 1905 the long farming reign ended abruptly. By order of the mortgagees the 185 acre Agricultural Estate "comprising a comfortable Old-Fashioned Farm House" was put to auction in Norwich on 15 July. Spread through Strumpshaw, Lingwood, Blofield and Buckenham were arable fields, pastures, various buildings including a "Famous Large Brick-and-Thatched Barn and seven labourer's cottages". The new owner would be subject to various Quit and Corn Rents to the Manors of Strumpshaw, Braydeston and Blofield and Black's Charity: "1 coomb of wheat sent to the Church Porch, the day after Christmas to be distributed". In all there were eight lots.

At the auction held in the Board Room of the Agricultural Hall, Norwich, Lot 1 was the largest at 130 acres. It comprised of the old house with numerous enclosures and buildings and was bought by Charles Mills, a railway signalman of Lingwood, who by 1896 had established himself as a shopkeeper. His shop site today is occupied by Lingwood's Spar stores close by the junction of the two villages.

In 1916 the Mills' adopted, as their child, a baby girl Kathleen, born in Great Yarmouth. Kathy Mills

By order of the Mortgagees.

NORFOLK.

STRUMPSHAW, LINGWOOD, BLOFIELD & BUCKENHAM

HIGHLY IMPORTANT

Agricultural Estate,

COMPRISING A COMFORTABLE

OLD-FASHIONED FARM HOUSE,

WITH

RIDING STABLE AND GIG HOUSE;

Extensive and Modern Agricultural Premises,

TOGETHER WITH

NUMEROUS ENCLOSURES OF VERY FERTILE ARABLE & PASTURE LAND,

SEVEN LABOURER'S COTTAGES,

FOUR VALUABLE ENCLOSURES of ACCOMMODATION ARABLE LAND,

Well adapted for Market Gardening purposes;

TWO WELL-SITUATED MARSHES,

THE WHOLE CONTAINING

185a. 2r. 38p.,

For many years occupied by Mr. T. Atkins, which

SALTER, SIMPSON & SONS

ARE FAVOURED WITH INSTRUCTIONS TO SELL BY AUCTION, AT

THE BOARD ROOM, AGRICULTURAL HALL, NORWICH,

On Saturday, July the 15th, 1905,

AT TWO O'CLOCK PRECISELY.

IN EIGHT LOTS.

Particulars, Plan, and Conditions of Sale may be had on application to the Auctioneers, Attleborough, Norfolk, and Bury St. Edmunds, Suffolk; or from

Messrs. Fosters, Burroughes & Calvert,

Vendors' Solicitors, 2, Upper King Street, Norwich.

R. COLBY AND SON, PRINTERS, UPPER KING STREET, NORWICH.

Oaklands sale poster of 1905.

Charles and Anna Mills, at Oaklands, May 1926, with Kathy Mills and Harry Turner.

Kathy Mills.

An Albion self binder in the field behind The Goat c1935.

Kathy Mills and Harry Turner in the bullock yard at Oaklands c1923.

A very early binder in Strumpshaw, c1915, with Harry Rose at the wheel.

grew up on the farm to become familiar with the seasons and witness the gradual mechanisation of the farming processes. Oaklands was a mixed farm, rearing livestock and rotating its crops. Root growing had come to prominence since the opening of the country's first sugar factory at neighbouring Cantley in 1912.

Ripening corn which had been growing on Strumpshaw's farms since its sowing the previous winter was ready to harvest in July and August. It was cut and tied into bunches called sheaves and stood up all over the field in clumps of eight or ten. Kathy Mills remembered the self-binder reaping the harvest, being drawn by two horses, during the school summer holiday which was generally referred to as "the harvest holiday":

2009, Maureen Jenkins tends the walnut sapling grown from the tree planted in memory of Charles Mills in 1943.

tions he stayed with the farm until his death in 1943 and in his time became a creditable member of the community being elected a Parish and District Councillor. Oaklands was inherited by Charles Mills' nephew, Frank Futter who increased its size to 160 acres.

When Charles Mills died, the Futter family planted a walnut tree to his memory in the stackyard. The young walnut was transplanted from Charles' own orchard. In 1978 it was engulfed by the landscaping of Beech Drive's gardens but had to be felled after 60 years when it obstructed new building work. But the lineage survives by a sapling, grown from a nut of the tree, found close by, in the store of a resident squirrel!

In the days of mixed farming Strumpshaw was home to a celebrated Irish cattle dealer. Frank Coady lived at Hill Rise from where he visited the markets of Birkenhead, Rugby, Leicester, Bury and Norwich and used to import up to 8000 head of Irish cattle into this country every year. Arthur Carter worked as one his drivers and recalled Frank complaining about having to pay four shillings (20p) a head of cattle carried by railway from Birkenhead to Norwich. This was more than his shipping charges from Ireland to England.

'I loved the summer holiday because I used to go in the harvest field, and of course the harvest field went over the railway bridges as well. I used to lead the horses to take an empty cart up to the field, ride them sometimes, then bring the full cart back. Of course there was an art in building a stack and the men used to say 'you can stop that job now and come and stand Bully'. Standing bully, means you stood between the man on the wagon, who was passing the sheaves of corn to the man on the stack. I would have to stand between them, catching the sheaf on my fork and passing it to the other. I really loved the harvest time. They used to have a long wagon to cart the corn and a 'morphy', meaning hermaphrodite. It was a pair of wheels and a board which turned a trumbril into a wagon for the harvest. It was neither one thing nor the other!'

The freshly cut sheaves of corn were brought and stacked in the stack-yard, in what is now Beech Drive. The stacks were built on to a base of hedge trimmings, cut by the men at the end of May, as the corn stacks were never put down on the bare ground. The long stalks of straw bearing the heads of precious grain would wait for threshing in the winter months

Within living memories, Charles Mills was denounced as a "speculator". Whatever his aspira-

On the far side of the village the harvest was also being brought in at Old Hall Farm. The men took the work on a contract, an agreed price to get the crops in. It was the one time when farm labourers could make extra money. If they got the job done in short time it was to their advantage. John Beck was the Team-man for Albert Key on the Old Hall Estate. He was driving horses in Beighton fields at the age of ten:

'We had a sail reaper with two horses and three on a binder and if it was a very hilly field you might have four. One out in front; I'd be the boy riding the trace horse on the binder which would have two horses on the for the first round of the crop because you couldn't get three horses to turn the corners. After the first round you'd put the other horse on and keep going round and round'.

outgoings demanded by the Lords of the Manor. During the First World War, with food constraints being in place, the handout was made in bread: "which was much appreciated by the parishioners". This happened again during the Second World War.

Year after year the people came to the porch but gradually the poor shrunk in number. In 1957 the occasion attracted press comment on celebrating the 200th distribution. By now it was mostly the same group of people who turned out, sometimes on a chilly day. Frank Futter was the occupant, at what was now Oaklands, and son, Frank junr. would deliver the wheat:

'The thing says it should be grown on the farm and it should be the best wheat. That didn't always happen. It was not always grown on the farm. We had wheat but sometimes it would have been sold as father had forgotten to save a sack-full. He used to curse, 'Oh sod it, we'll get one in', so he bought one in. Once or twice there were grumbles, it was not the best wheat, it was grotty stuff. I used to stick the wheat on my little car trailer and take it up to the church and with some help push it right up to the church porch. People were waiting, the same ones every year, the churchwardens ready with hand-cups to dish it out. Harold Broom was there as well as Digger Saunders'.

Betty Warman was present too, and on one occasion not pleased. Frank Futter had brought "some really awful stuff" and husband Lewis reckoned it was not wheat. He would have known, being a farmer, it was like "throw away barley, it was really gross". Christine McNamara, daughter of the last blacksmith was a regular:

'I used to take two bags, one lot for my grandmother who lived at the forge and one for me. She didn't always have the corn as she'd let me have it for the birds. A lot of people, like my grandmother, used to keep a few chickens and for the first ten years of my married life I kept a few hens so the corn was useful'

At some time in its history the William Black benefaction was drawn into the fold of the Charity Commissioners. In 1983 they considered the provision of corn was no longer an effective method of relieving poverty and tempted fate by suggesting that revenue could be raised and put to better use including linking them to the other village charities. Anyway, the amount of corn was trifling and the Charity Commissioners had not reckoned for the wrath of Strumpshaw! The William Black distribu-

tion survives to this day!

During the time of Thomas Atkins' occupation of William Black's estate another Strumpshaw charity was instituted. A fuel allotment or Poor's Marsh comprised in an Inclosure Award dated around 1810 was made in connection with the Strumpshaw and Surlingham Inclosure Act. This gave 10 acres and 2 roods, allotted to the Lord of the Manor, the rector and the churchwardens and overseers as trustees for the poor of Strumpshaw. Traditionally, the income from grazing or the sale of hay from the marsh was used to provide coal for the poor. Four trustees were eventually appointed by the parish council when the local government act of 1894 came into place. In January 1895 a total of 22 tons of coal was distributed amongst forty five families, the amounts ranging from 3 to 10 hundredweights or sacks-full.

More fuel for the fires of Strumpshaw's poor was added through the will of William Charles Flower Holmes in 1924. His father owned the Strumpshaw estate from 1881 and William's bequest was £500 to the Rector and Churchwardens to invest the sum and use the income to provide coal for the needy of the parish.

Now with virtually no demand for coal the constitution has been reworked to give money to pensioners for any needy situation who might be seen as fit to benefit. Money is distributed on a regular basis with some retained for emergencies. The Poor Marsh remains active with rent coming in plus a payment from DEFRA.

Another charitable movement instigated the parish's first public building. It began in 1896 when James Pryke, a retired shopkeeper of Lingwood sold a piece of his land for £5 to a committee of local men. John Cooper and Charles Mills of Lingwood along with Frank Neave and George Rope of Strumpshaw

Dressed for the parts at the corn distribution, 26 December 2005. Left to right: Elizabeth Cameron, Iris Gale, David Varley, Ann Varley, Gloria Fagg.

The St John's Ambulance Brigade, Reading Room, c1979. The photograph includes: Fred Rope, Vic Mayes, Anne & Keith Seaman, Jimmy Hubbard, Alison Long, Doreen Saunders, Neville Burton, Joan Tubby, Dennis Yaxley, Charlie Smith.

Mother's Union members in the Parish Room. Left to right: Joan Barrie, Ethel Wright, Doris Wright, Gladys Cormack, Margaret Rope.

Strumpshaw & Lingwood Reading Room, 2009.

Strumpshaw Parish Room serving as the Polling Station for local and European elections in 2009.

and James Pryke pledged to erect a Reading Room in Chapel Road:

'To be used by the inhabitants of the said parishes of Lingwood and Strumpshaw as a reading and news-paper room and library and for any other purposes of a public or private nature and for exhibitions, public meetings, concerts, lectures and other entertain-ments'.

The men set about collecting subscriptions to pay for the land and build the room. It was quite an under-taking but the aim was achieved with the foundation stones laid on 24th January 1898 by Charles Edmund Gooch of Burlingham and James William Holmes of Strumpshaw Hall. The hall served its purpose and a new group of trustees were appointed in 1941; Percy Loynes, Maurice Youngs, Bertie Beales, Frank Futter, Cecil Rope and Albert Key. In 1955, William Futter of Fern House, neighbour of the room, conveyed a small piece of land to enable the addition of toilets and drainage.

For more than forty years much of the room's manage-ment was handled by Jack Edwards of Lingwood. He came to the village at the age of ten "in 1912 the flood year" when his father's job on the railway brought them to live in Strumpshaw's crossing cottage on the gates at Goat Lane. Jack became involved with the village's social life which centred on the Reading Room run then by Bob Goodrum. There were two billiard tables and dominoes was a favourite. Billiards was organised into a local league which took Jack

John Barnes who farmed Hollies Farm until 1864.

and the other chaps cycling to play at Reedham, Freethorpe and Filby whose teams paid return visits to Chapel Road. Jack recalled the time when two of the 'top ones' in the first team were Joe Cushings, "who had the paper round the other side of the village" and Frank Futter.

After eighty five years of service the building showed signs of wear. To meet the requirements of new legislation the room's supporters implemented the Reading Room Restoration Fund and gradually brought the building to modern standards. With their devotion the building remains a testimony to the original trustees of 1896.

Strumpshaw's most recent benefactors were the Barnes' family. They were well rooted here in the 17th century and exercised a caring spirit in the later times until they passed without issue in 1968. The family's charitable work became active when Edward Barnes and his wife came to the village to help run the farm of his aging uncle, John Tuck Barnes. Strumpshaw became their permanent home where they raised four daugh-ters and pledged a whole hearted life to the church.

Edward Barnes died in 1898 and after the passing of Mrs Barnes in 1914 their children planned a memorial. Daughters Mary, Anne, Margaret and Catherine donated a plot from their father's, Hollies Farm for a parish room in 1915. The room, built by John Gedge of Blofield was a gift to the people of Strumpshaw, for their use, but from the beginning there were strings attached. These were made clear, later, through an indenture dated 7 October 1922.

The stated uses covered most events that were likely to be held in such a village hall. There was no barring of any particular groups but most important was the management. The Rector and churchwardens would forever be the trustees and they would sanction any charitable work or purpose in the hall which they thought proper for the people of Strumpshaw. The powers were made clear that the parish room stayed with the church. The trustees, that is the rector and churchwardens, might see fit to: "let, sell, pull down, rebuild" but not without the consent in writing of the Bishop of the Diocese of Norwich.

Throughout the Parish Room's history only the occasional hiccup occurred. These came mostly with a change of incumbent and a fresh argument over who actually owned the building. Wesley Key, who married the only grand-daughter of Edward Barnes, was involved in one heated incident:

'They had another peculiar parson here. He was a rum old boy. The parish room had a big notice board which Miss Barnes had bought and paid for. She'd got permission off Charlie Mills to fix it on his wall, so he claimed it. Well the parson, he claimed it, but Miss Barnes said it was hers. So one night I went and got it off Charlie's wall and nailed it on the parson's gate. I got two ruddy great iron nails and drove them through the top bars. There was a hell of a row kicked up about it and the police were trying to find who done it. Miss Barnes said it was hers so after about three or four days I took it off the parson's gate and nailed it on her front door. They never did find out who it was!'

To legal minds the parish room truly belongs within the fold of the church. The indenture of 1922 even prepared for its future:

'If at any future time the relative positions between Church and State shall be altered so that the Church and her possessions would become the property of the State such alteration shall not in any way affect or interfere with the premises hereby conveyed but the same shall remain vested in the Trustees and not be under State control'

So there!

Strumpshaw Youth Club in October 1969. Left to right, back row: Christine Church (seated), David Rose, David Sewell. Front: Martin Church, Dawn Riley, Sheila Greenfield. (PICTURE BY COURTESY OF EASTERN DAILY PRESS)

Chapter 8

◇

The Mill on the Hill

'There is a remarkable windmill in this town supposed to stand upon the highest ground in Norfolk; it is seen at a vast distance and overlooks most of the neighbouring hundreds; from it Yarmouth and Lowestoft in Suffolk are easily distinguished and it has full command of the city of Norwich, not being distant above seven miles. Being situated near Buckenham Ferry, there is a delightful view of the river Yare meandering through the country till it falls into Breydon Broad near Yarmouth. The prospect from this windmill is the finest coup d'oeil in the county of Norfolk and the mill itself when the sails are going is a beautiful object as far as it can be seen'

This was how Mostyn Armstrong described Strumpshaw's most prominent landmark in his *History and Antiquities of the County of Norfolk* in 1781. So moved was he by what he saw on his visit, only a French description sufficed for that instant opening of his eyes.

Strumpshaw mill was demolished in 1916. The very high ground on which it was built; an eminence of gravel thrown up during the ice age, led to its downfall. In the latter part of its productive life the surrounds were gradually quarried, being a valuable source of sand and gravel. Eventually the mill was undermined as the excavations encroached from the south and west to leave it standing on a pinnacle which made the structure unsafe. The end was hastened by the installation of steam power to drive the milling machinery.

Bowen's 1749 map of Norfolk was the first to show the mill. Although the "highest ground in Norfolk" is suspect, it did stand at 130ft above sea level. One description insists it was 146ft but it is safely described as standing on the highest ground in the parish and certainly the highest hill between Norwich and Great Yarmouth. Today, the contour is more like 128ft on the restored ground of the former quarry.

In windmill technology it was a ten-sided smock mill, an age old description as it resembled a shepherd's smock. Strumpshaw's mill was built to grind

Strumpshaw Mill c1910 seen from Mill Hill, looking west toward Norwich, the wooded horizon far left.

Strumpshaw Mill very close to the cliff-edge c1915.

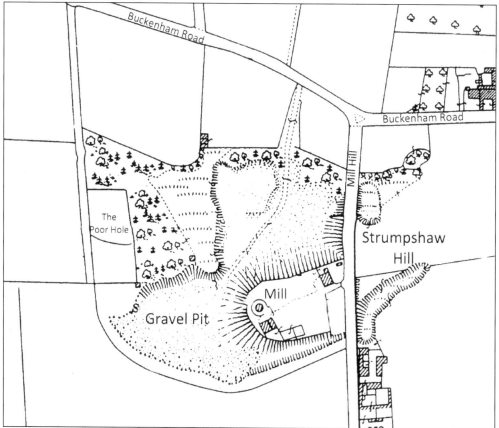

The position of Strumpshaw Mill, c1907.

grain into flour for bread or courser material for animal fodder. The wind was harnessed by its four double-shuttered sails, with eight bays of three and one of two. The top had a boat shaped cap with a straight ridge. As implied, it resembled an up-turned rowing boat, clinker style. At the rear was a chain pole and fan tail, the means by which the sails were moved to face the wind.

When Strumpshaw was mapped for the Enclosure Act in 1822, the mill site was attributed to William Pyle. The lands of Robert Walpole and John Tuck Barnes encompassed the parcel of land occupied by the mill. From 1836 it was managed by various tenant millers, with some coming in to Strumpshaw from other mills in the county. The Norfolk Chronicle advertised the vacant mill in June 1860: "To be let: For a term of years from Michaelmas next, Strumpshaw Mill. Enquire of A. L. Womack, Mettingham, Bungay.

In 1881 most of the site around, including the mill, was acquired by William Holmes during his purchase of the Strumpshaw Hall Estate. He set about keeping the mill in good order with the help of local millwrights, Smithdales of Acle. During 1882 they supplied a Stone Spindle, 1 Stone Box, 2 Wall Plates and 1 chimney Ring. A year later, the mill was taken by miller William Littleproud, who also served as baker and beer retailer.

Steam appeared in 1896 under the tenancy of Frederick William Kemp. Having started with the trade in 1868 he brought a lifetime of milling experi-

ence to Strumpshaw after working the mills at Elsing, Witton, Croxton and Ovington. Frederick raised his family in the mill house, with sons Alfred and Victor serving in the first war, while daughter Florence went to London as a nurse.

When Frederick Kemp retired, the mill continued with Frank Neave in 1904, who was already farming in the village. By 1908 the mill was becoming derelict, steam was taking over, and Frank Neave was running a milling business in the granary at Lingwood Station yard. One of the last people to recall the mill working was Alice Manthorpe. As a little girl she often went there and recounted one occasion, coming close to serious mishap:

'I remember the corn being carted to the mill. I was nearly killed. I was on a tumbril and the sails came round and my uncle shouted to me to drop down. I was a good girl; I dropped down otherwise I should have been dropped down by the sails coming round. I lived on the farm at the bottom of the hill and midway was Frank Neave the corn merchant and miller and up at the top was the clerk of the works. He had a daughter Sybil and we used to take it in turns to visit each other's. That's where I spent my young days'

When the mill was demolished in 1916 most of the timber went to Salhouse for reuse. The materials were useful in this period of shortages during the first war. It was a sad time for many who were

Stephen John Batchelder's watercolour of Strumpshaw Mill, 1912.

delighted by the sight Strumpshaw's familiar landmark. Farmer, Clifford Youngs had often watched the sails of the mill turning from Blofield. Arthur Grint's father, Barney, could spot the sails turning, if the sun was glinting at the right angle, as he entered Yarmouth harbour when returning from a period of fishing on his drifter.

Only for the legacy of photographers and artists could today's generations appreciate what had moved Moyston Armstrong to describe Strumpshaw Mill. Stephen John Batchelder 1849-1932, noted for his broadland scenes, rendered two watercolours, not long before the mill was demolished. John Arnesby Brown 1866-1955, who worked from a studio in Haddiscoe, and now compared to Alfred Munnings, delivered his impression of the mill about the time he was admitted to the Royal Academy. He was knighted in 1938. More recently, was Arthur Edward Davies, 1893-1988 with a distinctive watercolour. The works of all three artists fetch good prices in today's salerooms.

The Mill House survived the gravel working's onslaught until c1966. After the mill's demolition the well appointed building became home to a succession of tenants, mostly for people employed in the quarry. In 1922 came Graham Cotman, whose great uncle John Sell Cotman was the famed artist of the Norwich School of painters. Graham achieved acclaim as an architect with Edward Boardman in Norwich. The Mill House, on its commanding high ground provided home to Shepherd and Hilda Goodwin with their family.

Shepherd and Hilda Goodwin who made The Mill House their family whom for some years.

Strumpshaw Mill: a retrospective view by Martin Sexton.

◇

Chapter 9

The Best Days of Their Lives

Children going to school in the Strumpshaw of 1845 may have been born lucky. The only place of tuition was Miss Wells' Boarding School, of just six pupils of 6-12 years, as children at that time of day were not forced to be educated. Miss Wells tutored in what today we know as Church Cottage assisted by Strumpshaw born teacher, Charlotte Thompson.

Compulsory education came in 1870 when inspectors scoured the land in search of sites to build Board Schools. The building had to be within walking distance of the pupils and that could be some distance when comparing the amount of walking done today. Strumpshaw's site was selected from land owned at the time of the enclosures by Thomas Tuck of the Hall Estate.

The School Board of five members was formed on 19 May 1873 to serve the districts of Strumpshaw, Braydeston and Brundall. This is why the school was built close to the boundary of all three parishes and some way from the main village. Bradeston population was 133 in 1865 and Brundall 104, together not matching Strumpshaw's 386.

The new school was built by John Withers of Blofield to a design by J B Pearce of Norwich. It opened with a short religious service at 11am on 12 October 1874 in the presence of Revd Whitbread, rector at the time and Edward Barnes one of the village's major landowners. Strumpshaw's school was built to hold one hundred children but the average number of pupils was seventy five.

Strumpshaw School, c1930.

Attendance at the new school may have been compulsory but it was not free. The Act of Parliament ruled that children attending the new board schools would have to pay a fee. Strumpshaw's rate varied from 2 to 8 pennies (1p to 3p approx) for each pupil per week but most of them were charged 4d (just under 2p today). The school board took decisions on whether to allow children of very poor parents to be taught without charge.

The early curriculum was very formal with little chance of pupils following their own interests. Punishment figured largely and could even be metered out for something which happened outside of school-time. There was an incident in July 1878 when a gentleman complained of boys scaring his riding horses in Long Lane. They had innocently been cracking their whips on farm horses, they were riding as hol'yer boys, an out of school occupation, which had resulted in the other horses being scared. Children were allowed some days absence from school to help with the harvest. The 'culprits' were thrashed at school next day and given a strict talk by the rector and one of the school board members.

Harry Thompson, who grew up to become known as 'Buncher', was punished at the request of his grandmother for refusing to go to school one morning:

'He received two strokes of the cane on each hand, in the presence of the assistants only'

In 1895 when the headmistress was Mrs Hogg a visit from Her Majesty's Inspector on 31 January resulted in a good report. The weather was bitter and attendance was good in the 'mixed school', held in the larger room:

'The children are in very good order and the instruction was very creditable. Handwriting deserves special mention, the paper-work being extremely neat. In the infant's class, many children were absent, owing to the stormy weather. There is a very good tone in this department. The order and instruction are creditable'

Forever on the agenda of the Parish Council was the election of school managers. In 1903 Mr J C Waters was elected from the village to act with the four already chosen by the County Council: James Owen Holmes of Strumpshaw Hall, T Slipper, Thomas Atkins and Rev Chamberlain.

Doris Batchelor joined the junior class in 1926 when it was separated from the seniors by a curtain. There were no half-term holidays, just Easter, Summer and Christmas. With other friends she walked the winding Long Lane to school from home

Strumpshaw School, c1900, one of the oldest known photographs of pupils.

Class 3, Strumpshaw School, 1929. Left to right, back row: ?, ?, ?, Joe Fox, Ivor Lumley. Third row: Miss Royal, Fred Barrett, Laurence Bedford, Tom Stone, Percy Fuller, John Spooner, ?, Billy Cook, Dick Fox, Tom Simpson, Lewis Grint. Second row: ?, Nora Wilby, Iris George, Irene Collins, Edna Cowles, Kathy Horner, ?, Maggie Horner, Gladys Barber, Olive Curtis, Agnes Wilby, Doris Batchelor. Front row: Sybil Williamson, Cissy Fox, Elsie Church, Muriel Church, Nora Church, Alice Rose, Peggy George, ?, Phylis Ashley, Cissy Atkins, ?, Emily Barrett.

in Buckenham Road, having to contend with sugar beet lorries during the campaign times. After the morning's lessons they would walk back home for lunchtime and return for the afternoon session until finishing at 3-45pm.

A highlight for Doris was a nature walk. Miss Royal would take the class from the school and up Stone Road as far as The Grove, an attractive wooded area on the right hand side, to be shown all that was growing there. It was the only outing in those days and they thought it was out of this world.

Ruby Stone, an eight year old, came with her family to live in Strumpshaw and looked back on the time as the happiest of her life. In her years at the school the headmistress was Miss E Lester with two teachers, Miss Royal who taught the juniors and Miss Payne the infants:

'The Christmas parties at Strumpshaw School come back to mind. For weeks before Christmas, Miss Royal taught us carols and special Christmas songs. A concert was arranged by the teachers and we were allowed to invite our parents. We had a feast in the large classroom which housed the juniors and seniors in those days. Miss Lester, the headmistress, prepared all the lovely things we had to eat; jellies, cakes, sandwiches and sausage rolls. And we always had crackers. She must have paid for this herself as we never gave anything towards this lovely feast. After the carols and tea Miss Lester brought forth the presents and we all had a gift from a huge sack'

Betty Warman never liked Strumpshaw school but she managed to progress its stages. The infants class took ages five to seven followed by the junior and senior classes, and she recalled being separated by the curtain. Winters were made comfortable by a blazing fire:

'There were no secretaries or anything like that. We did have a lady go in every night to clean and clear out the grates. We had Horlicks to drink. I can remember having this enormous urn of Horlicks for which we paid tuppence h'penny a week (1p in decimal currency). Peter Ashley always had two as there wasn't very much in a cup. We had milk, not at the same time, and when the weather was really cold, it froze, and pushed up the cap'

The most evocative period within living memory of Strumpshaw school started in 1944 with the arrival of Barbara Buckton, the new headmistress. Originally from Durham, she and her seven year old son David had been blitzed out of their home at Little Melton the previous year:

'1944 was the time when everyone at school had to have their gas mask with them. When the siren sounded we had to evacuate the school quickly, to go into a shelter, built by the parents when Mr Jennings was headmaster. It was a brick lined 'cave' dug into the field of Mr Hewitt's, High noon Farm. Three times we had to leave dinners half-eaten and go back when the 'all-clear' signal was given. At that time, dinners were supplied in metal containers from an Army Meals Centre in Acle. The school's big kitchen was not built until fifteen years later when we supplied Postwick, Buckenham and Plumstead School's meals, transported by Billy Tidman of Brundall. Also in 1944, Connie Atkins and Josie Cunningham helped Mrs Rose, the caretaker, everyday, to wash up the dinner items and there were over 100 children when we included the evacuees from Dagenham. For these we had to use the Parish Room as a classroom. Mrs Snelling walked the children in crocodile fashion down Long Lane for dinner and afterwards walked them back'

Soon after Barbara Buckton's arrival it was time for the education of Noel Hewitt. His father's High Noon Farm was the school's neighbouring property so the route for young Noel was just down Cuckoo Lane. But Noel mastered the means of a quick retreat when he had enough of Mrs Buckton:

'I used to nip over the back wall of the school and

Mrs Dann's class c1946. Left to right, back row: ?, Raymond Brown, Gerald Woolston, Ray Driver, Mrs Dann. Front row: ?, Gillian Clavert, Beryl Barret, Noel Hewitt, ?, Madeline Rose, Janet Cunningham.

Mrs Snelling's class, 1946. Left to right, back row: Pat Moore, John Shingles, ?,?, Reggie Tortoise, Mrs Snelling. Middle: Trevor Bennett, ?, John Kent, ?,?,?,?. Front row: Beryl Woolston, Shirley Jermy, Shirley Hewitt, Sally Curtis, Pauline Sage, Daphne Hewitt, Jean Rose.

come across the fields, cross the railway line and then through the pasture and home. I didn't like school from the day I went to the day I left. Poor old father and Sid Curtis would be watching. I think one morning he took me back three times. In the end, I spent the morning in her arms. She wouldn't let me go so I had to tolerate school after that. I've got no bad memories of Mrs Buckton. She was stern and fair. She was well thought of. We were taught the basics and everything else'

One little girl who did stay in school and took to her work seriously was Patricia Watson. In 1940 at the age of seven her conduct was "Very good" and she achieved marks of 101 out of a possible 140. The headmaster at the time was Mr Jennings and Pat's education continued under the headship of Mrs Buckton in 1944. By 1952 Patricia had moved to Norwich Training College as a student teacher and after graduating, taught at Thorpe Hamlet and Lingwood schools.

When the winters were far colder the walk from village to school could be treacherous. Jean Childs

Patricia Watson marries Hylton Nichols at Strumpshaw in December 1956.

(née Beardwood) started her attendance in 1957 and found the regime of Mrs Buckton quite comfortable and the school never closed, even during the worst weather:

Strumpshaw School group of 1957. Left to right, back row: Tony Lake, Eric Shingles, Allan Sussans, Michael Beck, Christopher Bartram, Rodney Riley, Tony Ashley. Third row: Andrew Stone, George Dungar, Linda Baker, Linda Everson, Pat Petter, Barry Everson, Barry Futter. Second row: Daphne Tortoise, Carol Piggin, Patricia Roberts, Mrs Buckton, Dorothy Wooler, Diane Rose, Jennifer Wooler. Front row: Derek Smith, Michael Turner, Brian Cunningham, Roger Baker, Christopher Futter, David Barrett, Frankie Hewitt.

Strumpshaw School Nativity play, 1966. The photograph includes: Gillian Marriot, Timothy Cianchi, Martin Adams, Billy Ridley, Jennifer Knox, Gloria Simmons, Patricia Patterson, Susan Buttrum, Kevin Marriot, Douglas Patterson, Susan Turner, Peter Stone, Sarah Knox, Stewart Adams, Raymond Forder, Susan Fox, Christine Church, Fred Patterson, Linda Roofe, Sheryl Roofe, Julie Edwards and Brenda Trice.

Strumpshaw School sports, c1949. Left to right, back row: Anne Stevens, Jean Rose, Gerald Woolston, Patrick Moore, Raymond Driver, Tony Bartam, Roger Monkman, Shirley Jermy, Evelyn Knights. Centre: ?, Daphne Rose, Mary Nurse, Gloria Webb, Brenda Beck, Janet Cunningham, Sally-Anne Buckingham, Madeline Rose, Raymond Baker. Front: David Frost, Noel Hewitt, Sandra Dyball, ?, Jennifer Smith, George Smith, ?.

'The Long Lane banks were piled fifteen feet high. To a small child it was like walking through mountains, always completely blocked off with snow in winter. So we walked over the fields, the three of us, Sheila Greenhill, Dawn Riley and me. We used to make for the three trees and then cut across to the road. One of us, always, would fall in a drift. We used to get there and Mrs Buckton would have a big blazing fire and a crate of milk. The milk would be popping out of the top, where the ice had swelled'

An energetic dance during the pageant of 1957.

Michael Turner and his classmate, Mickey Monkton never quite had the same comfortable time with Mrs Buckton. One hot summer's day they tried to abscond but were soon hauled back, to have their legs tied together, to the leg of the desk.

Strumpshaw school could present hazards of another kind. Until a dedicated playing field was in place the pupils were given the use of Tom Hewitt's neighbouring pasture for shinty, football and anything requiring a grass pitch. The added skill was avoiding the cowpats!

Getting to school down Long Lane had added thrills in the 1950's. The entire length of the road was excavated for the laying of mains water which gave Tony Atkins and two friends the chance to get to school by walking in the bottom of the trench, as far as possible, without being seen. There was no shut-

Strumpshaw School pupils performing the pageant, 1957.

tering; it was totally dangerous, the stuff of real boyhood days.

Strumpshaw School Sports c1950. Left to right, back row: John (Ted) Stevens, John Kent, David Lynn, Cynthia Flowerdew, Pauline Sage, Janice Moore, Beryl Woolston, Jean Rose. Centre: Gerald Woolston, Anne Stevens, Joyce Lynn, Daphne Lock, Jill Payne, Evelyn Knights, Patrick Moore. Front: Raymond Broom, Brenda Beck, Mary Nurse, Janet Cunningham, Tony Atkins, Stephen Wright, Gilbert Cawley.

Mrs Buckton became integrated into the village community. She founded the Strumpshaw Players in 1946, the village's drama group which performed in the Old Barn and joined the Parochial Church Council as secretary. A highlight in 1957 was her masterminding of a celebration of the church's 700th anniversary; a colourful pageant performed by the schoolchildren. On another occasion a Punch & Judy show was staged at the school and Sheila Ashford took son Andrew along:

'I had taken my three and half year old son to see the show. Imagine my horror the very next day when I couldn't find him in our garden. After frantically searching the near neighbourhood I came home in tears, to receive a telephone call to say that he was at the school! He had walked down the dangerous Long Lane and announced that he wanted to go to school. Well, why not? School meant Punch & Judy shows'

The recollections of Strumpshaw's schooldays were generally good, at that time of day when pupils respected their teachers. Most pupils went into the world and achieved, more or less what they expected. Two notables were Mrs Buckton's son David, who became Curator of the British Museum's Early Christian and Byzantine collections; and Clive Jermy, author and leading authority on ferns and mosses.

Clive Jermy, Tony to his family, started at Strumpshaw School in 1937 when Mr Jennings was headmaster. The infant teacher Miss Royal set him off in life and Barbara Buckton's gift of a book, Rev John's Flora, launched his botanical career. Passing the 11+ examination took Clive to the City of

Strumpshaw School "dinner ladies" in 1979. Left to right, back: Mary Forder, Sandra Church and Barbara Fox.

Norwich School then on to University College London and eventually to Leicester University. After a teaching spell at Gravesend Grammar School he became responsible for the Fern Section at the Natural History Museum and stayed for 30 years.

Clive's course of life had been nurtured in Strumpshaw. From his family home at Mauveen in Low Road it was a short trip to the family's favourite collecting site on the railway embankments for primroses, wild strawberries and oxeye daisies. He met nature's local celebrity, Ted Ellis on his rounds, down on the marshes for his own collections, usually fungi. Clive retired in 1992 and looked back on a wonderful time of growing up in Strumpshaw.

In March 1959 a reorganisation reduced Strumpshaw school to infants and junior pupils only. The occasion was marked by a reunion of former staff and pupils and visited by Jonah Barrington, a BBC radio celebrity of that time, who made recordings for transmission in a Midland Home Service programme. The occasion was attended by Miss Royal who had taught Clive Jermy.

After 1969 Strumpshaw's pupil numbers began to decrease when Brundall's own school opened. By the mid 1970's the pupil register had dropped to fifteen. With a similar state in other villages the education authority set about reorganising the local system which led to the school closing on 19 December1980. It was bought by Arthur Marriot and converted to living accommodation.

From that time on Strumpshaw children went to Brundall CP School or Lingwood First and Lingwood Junior School and subsequently on to the High Schools of Thorpe or Acle.

Strumpshaw school boys Christopher Rowland and Martin Adams launch their self-built dinghy, under the eye of headmaster Mr Hycock, c1970.

Arthur Carter and Charlie Nicholls (at the wheel), 1984.

Chapter 10

Goings on in the Shed with Helen Hall

The history of Strumpshaw is bound in the lives of its people. Conversations and recollections of days gone by lead invariably to the village's well-loved individuals, often known by nickname only. These people were remembered for the provision of a necessary service, their occupation or some amusing antic.

There was 'Darky' Harper who lived in Pack Lane. He was the local fish merchant who travelled door to door selling his wares. The cured fish he offered was smoked in the back garden, in a corrugated iron shed and in a hole so deep that when Fred Rope's grandfather went to live in the house the dangerous opening had to be filled.

The district nurse might come visiting, on her "cranky" old bike, that is for those who had paid the insurance fee of one shilling a year; five pence in today's money. Alice Manthorpe, the post-woman, once delivered an urgent request to the nurse by postcard, from one old lady in the parish but on return the nurse was far from happy:

"What do you think, Alice?" she said, "I knocked at the door and asked who was ill" and she said "Nobody. I've paid my shilling and you hadn't been to see me so I wanted my shilling's worth"

Just off Norwich Road in cottages on Oaklands Farm lived Bob Scott and Jimmy Goodrum. Next door neighbour was Charlie Brown, the village blacksmith. Bob and Jimmy cohabiting, "Two old bachelors" some used to say but these boys lived in a time when liberation was some way off. They survived the rigours of farm labouring; going anywhere that work was offered.

Bob and Jimmy were happy with their lifestyle and never went hungry or thirsty. Thirsts were quenched at The Goat or sometimes as far away as the aptly named Two Friends at Blofield Heath. They might walk into the pub and empty the last of their earnings from a little bag onto a table, perhaps raising 2/6 (12.5p) and say, "What can we get? Oh dear, just two halves. We'll have to go to work tomorrow".

Their work was often found on Oaklands Farm, at harvest time, where they worked alongside Tony Atkins. Bob and Jimmy would help to pile the wagon with sheaves of corn and while Tony had gone with the load, Bob would fall asleep:

'Jimmy would say, "come on Bob, we've got work to do". And I remember them one Sunday lunchtime, coming over the bridge in Hemblington Road. We were looking out over our gate and this bike came past, back wheel first, and there was Jimmy pushing the bike and Bob lurching behind, "Bloody thing won't go straight Bob". Halfway up the road Bob fell over the bike and Jimmy fell into the Rectory Woods. They were so drunk'

Jimmy might appear like a tramp during the week but come Sunday he dressed immaculately for church. Freshly laundered shirts were supplied by his sister who lived not far away. Hunger was kept at bay, on occasions, by trips to Great Yarmouth to stock up with fresh herring. As for keeping the house warm in winter they once removed the staircase and systematically burned it in the grate. They never slept upstairs again. Both were considered harmless and were never barred from anywhere; the kind of colourful characters now sadly missed by a whole generation.

When Durham-born Barbara Buckton arrived in Strumpshaw as the school's new headmistress in 1944 nothing had prepared her for her nearest neighbour 'Crump' Waters. His first name was Jack but to everyone he was always "Crump". Barbara, with her seven year old son David, enjoyed conversations over the garden fence by Crump's house, a black shed-like building at an address called The Mount. Crump lived there alone, as his wife had died, but had the company of his pigs and goats. The goats were grazed on the green, opposite the school and the pigs were allowed to go inside Crump's house.

Lily and Cecil Curtis in 1971. (PICTURE BY COURTESY OF EASTERN DAILY PRESS)

The Curtis family. Left to right: Cecil, Lily, Sally, Olive, Victor, c1945.

Mrs Buckton enjoyed Crump's advice and ramblings of Norfolk folklore but became increasingly concerned that talk always concluded with the same line, "I'll have to go; I've got Helen Hall to do in the shed".

Barbara was already aware that Crump was the man to call for certain services, like castrating a male cat: "Push the feller into a Wellington boot and use a razor blade on him". She became concerned for the well-being of one Helen Hall. After requesting a translation of Crumps's pay-off, the answer was simple, "I'll have to go as I've got hell an' all to do in the shed". Translated, there was much work to be done!

Crump was the village roadman, or length-man as the council knew him. His job was to maintain Long Lane in good order, sweeping away the debris and repairing potholes. The length of his patch stretched up Long Lane as far as The Goat and he collected his materials from the council depot in Lingwood. He swept the roads early in the mornings and kept the drains clear under Brundall railway bridge, unlike today where flooding often follows heavy downpours.

But the ascending Long Lane was not Crump's only uphill climb. His barrow and tools would often disappear, while his back was turned. Then someone allowed his goats to escape as they grazed on the roadside pasture. The culprits were young Terry Atkins and his friends:

'He kept four goats and we used to let them go. My god he used to play hell up with us. He never knew where his barrow was from one day to the next but he was a good old boy. If one of his goats went off we'd go and help him to catch it, then we'd let it off the next day!'

Crump had to contend with the children, walking the route between the village and school. The road has a history of cascading water during most downpours and in winter, the children's favourite pleasure was making little dams from whatever could be found by the road. The result was 'swishes' of water rerouting the flow and choice language from Crump who was then left to clear the spoils.

Close to where those Long Lane swishes ended their flow lived Cecil and Lily Curtis. They spent their childhoods at Cantley and married at Blofield in 1921. Cecil saw First World War service with promotion to Company Sergeant Major and earned a bonus of £100 by staying in the army after the Armistice. He saved the money and bought a plot of Strumpshaw land for £92 at the junction of Stone and Low Roads.

He engaged Underdowns of Blofield to build a bungalow on the site and in 1925 moved in with his family, naming the new home Olvic. The name was a fusion of their first children's names, Olive and Victor.

Cecil worked at Brundall Station as a Leading Porter for 50 years but Lily is the most remembered because she was the lady who 'did'. What she did was deliver babies and lay out the dead of the parish with total dedication whenever called upon. Her medical expertise was once used to put back a local chap's eyeball after it popped out during a strenuous bit of gardening. Much of Lily's experience was gained during the first war when she worked at St Andrew's Hospital helping to care for wounded soldiers brought back from France.

The Curtis's were industrious and public spirited. Another sideline was phoning through bets to Charles Nichols at the Shoulder of Mutton when Lily and Cecil were amongst the earlier telephone subscribers in Strumpshaw. During the 1940's they sold cigarettes and Sunday newspapers from their house and sweets for the children coming out of school.

Cecil was known to many around Strumpshaw as Crucian when he cycled on his rounds for hair cutting. A maroon, wooden box on his bike carried his clippers and scissors. He was a kindly man to his neighbours. Before retirement from the railway he cared for Frank Coady, a widower, living close by in a little wooden house. When Frank's wife passed on he would not allow any other woman into the house to clean and Cecil would assist him home to Strumpshaw from Brundall Station, if he happened to be the worse for a drink.

The most celebrated of Strumpshaw's nicknamed characters were the Thompson brothers, all four of them. There was "Wryneck Bob", "Twinner", "Sixer" and "Buncher" whose family home was in The Loke. Buncher was really Harry Thompson but like most of his namesakes, had been Baptised Henry. He achieved lasting notoriety through his mode of accommodation, an iron-wheeled shepherd's hut positioned just inside the stackyard of Oaklands farm, on the site now occupied by the first house in Beech Drive. Buncher lived out his life here, separated from his wife, managing a life of self sufficiency by growing vegetables, mainly onions and his own tobacco, plus a bit of poaching.

Frank Futter of Oaklands had allowed him to live there and in return he worked on the farm. Frank's grand-daughters, Carrol and Judy Piggin would visit him and recalled that the hut was always warm inside complete with the smell of the paraffin heater.

73

Terry Atkins could remember him working with the steam threshing contractors which leads to logic speculation of his affectionate name. He operated the buncher which was part of the threshing tackle. Betty Warman recalls passing at night and seeing him sitting by the window of the hut, smoking his pipe by the light of a candle, wondering to herself, "How could he ever live there?"

Sixer (George) Thompson, Buncher's brother, was born in the village in 1883 and lived here for all his life. Much of his time was employed as a cattle drover which meant he had walked miles over fields and roads around the area. His claim to fame was that at the age of 76 in 1959 he walked from the Shoulder of Mutton to the Norfolk Railway House pub in Norwich in less than two hours to win a £2 wager.

During the summertime Sixer would sit on the bank on Norwich Road, by Hill Rise, with 'Drover' Church, spending hours waving to passers-by. If any stranger stopped to enquire for directions to somewhere they simply answered: "Sorry, we're strangers". Sixer saw service in the first war and died in 1971 at the age of 88, and passed into history with the likes of 'Gravel Hole' Rose and 'Deadshot' Debbage.

Buncher Thompson's hut c1960 on the site which became 1 Beech Drive.

Chapter 11

Blacksmiths, Carpenters and Wheelwrights

Once upon a time Strumpshaw's blacksmith's forge and the carpenter's shop were places of fascination for children. Sparks would be flying, red hot iron was thrust spitting into cooling water and the potent odour as a hot shoe was placed scorching against the horse's hoof was all part of the attraction. In the carpenter's shop long curls of wood shavings would litter the floor having peeled away from the making of another coffin. In those days there were no health and safety issues. If children sensed danger they kept their distance.

For more than two hundred years the blacksmith's shop occupied its site at the junction of Hemblington and Norwich Roads. The blacksmith's forge was there for more than horses. Farm tools came in for repair, especially at harvest time, and in many cases the blacksmith had made the implement. A hundred years ago, the location was often referred to as Blacksmith's Corner and consisted of three cottages. Today, the attractive renovation of The Old Forge pays tribute to an industrious past.

One of the earliest references to Strumpshaw's 'smithy' appears in the Manor Court Book of 1770. A licence was granted to William Hylton to erect a building on land near his house. The Hyltons were a deep rooted Strumpshaw family and remained associated with the forge for several years. The 1809 Enclosure awards show Elizabeth Hylton claiming the black-

The Old Forge in 2007, formerly Strumpshaw's blacksmith.

Strumpshaw's blacksmith at the time of Robert Thrower c1900.

smith's shop. Further records show that in little more than 200 years of service there were few changes of blacksmith. The trade called for a tough and hardy race with skills being passed from father to son.

With recorded recollections back to 1874, Strumpshaw's forge was taken by Robert Thrower. He was born at Wickhampton, into one of England's most celebrated blacksmith families and came here with Eleanor his wife a Swanton Abbott girl and their two sons, Robert jnr and George. About the time Robert snr was born, one of his ancestral smiths from Hethersett made a set of horse-shoes to show at the Great Exhibition of 1851.

Robert and his family lived at Horning in 1873 and Crostwick before coming to Strumpshaw. Soon after settling here, another son, Thomas was born, but sadly he died, 22 March 1875, at the age of seven months. His gravestone carries his parent's last message:

'Rest darling rest in Thy gold bed of clay, Death came to thee early and took thy tender life away"

In 1894 Robert Thrower was present at the inauguration of the Parish Council. As a freeholder and subsequently a voter, Robert was eligible to nominate the chairman of the first meeting on 4 December that year. This was followed by the marriage of his son

George Thrower and his bride, Edith Rose, on their wedding day, May 1895. George was the younger son of Robert Thrower, and Edith, the sister of George Rose another blacksmith at the forge.

John Thrower, great grandson of Robert Thrower, at Strumpshaw in 2009.

Strumpshaw blacksmith c1945. Arthur Colman shoeing, with Tom Hewitt holding horse's back.

Robert Thrower with two of his children, July 1884.

George to Edith Rose in May 1895. Edith was the sister of George Rose a neighbour who also worked the forge with the Throwers. George Thrower took his wife to Saxlingham to become its blacksmith and when their son George was born, returned to Strumpshaw for the Baptism in August 1895. But Robert was hit by tragedy once more when Eleanor, his wife of more than thirty years, died 16 December 1902 aged 54.

The village shared in a bigger tragedy on 19 August 1909 when Robert Thrower was found to have taken his own life. The Deputy Coroner held an inquest at the Shoulder of Mutton on Friday 20 August. Neighbour and employee George Rose had been the last person to see Robert alive. He witnessed that the deceased came home between ten and eleven o'clock, in the evening of 18 August, having met with an accident by being thrown from his pony-trap near Hassingham. Two very bad cuts were bathed by George Rose who then assisted Robert into bed. Around midnight he bade him goodnight on agreement that he was happy to be left. In the morning Robert Thrower's door was found to be locked so a man named Hylton took a ladder and climbed to the bedroom window. There he discovered Robert hanging by a towel from a roof beam. It was thought he had been dead for about four or five hours. The jury returned a verdict of suicide whilst temporary insane.

This sad episode brought a change of ownership. The blacksmith's shop with its traverse, premises, land, three cottages and gardens was put for auction on Saturday 11 September 1909 at Norwich's Royal Hotel. In the event the property was bought by Richard Peart, of Lingwood, for his son Russel who

had been apprenticed to a Norwich chemist and wanted a healthier, outdoor occupation. He knew nothing of blacksmithing but luckily had struck up a friendship with Reggie Bunn, son of the Burlingham blacksmith, who worked with Richard Peart at Lingwood Station:

'Russel had got no experience at all and through my father having the Burlingham forge and me being here, we gave Russel the experience to take over. He had a brother Stanley. He was the posh one but Russel wasn't so posh. He was a lad, a born comedian really but him and his brother were like chalk and cheese. Stanley was very smart, not that Russel wasn't smart. Stanley just had that little bit extra'.

When the first war came Russel went off to the front with Reggie Bunn, but he never came back to the Strumpshaw forge. The work at the forge went on for the war's duration with employed smiths.

1916 brought another change of ownership with Arthur Colman and his son Herbert. Arthur was born at Smallburgh, Norfolk and in 1901 had been the Ingham blacksmith. The Colman's served the forge for a record fifty years and are remembered for introducing the first motor cars to the village. Herbert bought the first, a Standard, and his father followed with an Austin 12.

Arthur Colman's forge was never cold and it was a topical meeting place. He was always immaculate in collar and tie, working away while onlookers chatted: chaps or girls who had brought down horses to be shod. Arthur would never hear a wrong word about anybody. There was no gossip at his forge. Could you believe it?

There were five farms in the village and they relied heavily on horses lightening the work loads of the farm labourers. There were horses for ploughing, pulling wagons and binders and some attached to 'horse works' whereby the animal walked round in a circle, pulling on a beam to activate machinery in a barn. Eight or nine horses were kept at Oaklands Farm and all needed frequent shoeing.

On an average day Arthur would expect to shoe at least three horses before breakfast. If he woke to a rainy morning he was in for a busy time. With the horses not being able to work the fields they would be taken down to the blacksmith's for shoeing. This meant even more yarning. A neighbour of the forge was Mrs Benn, affectionately known as 'Clacker Benn' because of her incessant chattering or 'clacking', as it was known locally. She would lean over the wall separating her home from the blacksmith's shop, clacking to the men who had brought horses to be shod.

In 1925, sixteen year old Charlie Brown took a horse to the Colman's to be shod which led to him being engaged as an apprentice. The resident employee had been blinded in a shoeing accident caused by flying metal so had given up the work. Charlie stayed for lunch every day with Arthur and his wife, who was a good cook. She fed Charlie well which made him 'a big man', the requirement for a smith:

'Horses, you'd get all sorts. If they stood still the first time they never stood still any more all their life. If you got one that pulled you about a bit and you squared 'em up he always remembered and he'd stand better. If they were too much trouble you used to strap the front leg out and make them hop around the traverse on three legs. Youngs, the farmer, brought one down here from somewhere and she was a terror and I know I strapped her down and made her hop around on three legs. She got proper "woody" and laid down so I left her with the bloke and went home and had my breakfast. When I came back she was standing up again'.

Spring time was busy for Charlie and the Colman's. Shoeing horses continued along with the seasonal work of replacing worn tines in the harrows, ready for the spring cultivating. The forge was still going well up to the war although the old buildings were beginning to show their age. Since Herbert had taken

Charlie Brown at his works on the Beeches Barn site in 1981.

more interest in machinery, carpentry and wheel-wrighting Charlie had been assisted by Kenny Scot, a 'younker' (young fellow) who was called into the navy for war service. About this time Charlie was smitten by pneumonia and Arthur Colman became unable to work.

After recovery from pneumonia, Charlie was advised to work outside in the fresh air. He knew only of the trade of blacksmith so decided to become a mobile smith and go visiting. He set up his own forge on what had been Low Farm at The Beeches in Norwich Road toward Lingwood in premises acquired from Frank Futter. Charlie moved in and eventually took most of Colman's shoeing work.

Arthur Colman died in 1949 but son Herbert was never keen on shoeing horses. He made wheel-wrighting his speciality and operated in a workshop opposite The Shoulder of Mutton. He knew that mechanisation was gaining ground on horses so started an extension of the blacksmith's forge on the site now occupied by Brickfields, the housing development.

Henrietta Colman, Arthur's widow, who made a strong man of young Charlie Brown, died in March 1966 at the age of 84. She was well remembered by daughter-in-law Joyce:

'Mrs Colman didn't know what it was to go short. She never had any housekeeping money. All the money went in a drawer so she'd go there when she wanted something. She cooked Christmas puddings, mincemeat tarts and bread to give to the old folk who lived alone. She'd go to Norwich if she wanted a hat, and buy three. If she wanted a pair of shoes she'd buy three pairs of the very best. About a week after that, you'd see one shoe down the yard where she'd thrown it at the cat. She was a dear old soul but she was ever so untidy although she was never lonely. Everybody in the village would go there. When she was dying she said that she felt she'd had a good life and that her time had come'

Away from the heat of the village forge, wood was worked by Herbert Mayes, Strumpshaw's celebrated carpenter and builder. He moved to the area from Norwich to work in Albert Key's wheelwright and blacksmith's shop at neighbouring Beighton. When Albert came to farm at Strumpshaw Old Hall, Herbert Mayes and his son Herbert jun came too and set up business in the stack yard of Oaklands Farm, now the site of Beech Drive. They occupied a lean-to workshop, on what was a bullock shed, just inside on the right. At that time the yard was a timber store for wood imported from Russia for James Porter, a Norwich company.

Henrietta Colman (left) and Mrs Ridley.

Herbert Mayes senr and wife.

Herbert Mayes jnr and wife.

Bert Ridley, left, and Herbert Colman in Norwich Road by the entrance of what is now Brickfields, c1966.

Strumpshaw Engineering 1983, now replaced by Brickfields, looking toward Norwich Road.

Philip Armes, visiting farrier from Upton, shoeing Chester at Strumpshaw in 2007.

Neville Burton at Strumpshaw Engineering in 1982.

The cottage of Christopher Plow, Strumpshaw's shoemaker in the 19th century.

Herbert's workshop was one of the first to be fitted with electric light in the early 1930's when the mains power was brought to Strumpshaw. But the engineers never fitted a meter and after fifteen years the supply company discovered the error and tried to charge Herbert. He stubbornly refused and the electricity supplier had to give in.

The Mayes' business ranged from wheelwrights, as there still plenty of horse drawn carts and wagons in the parish, through to being the undertaker. Coffins made there in their workshop could often be seen being transported on a horse and cart, draped in black cloth on route to Homeleigh, the workhouse at Lingwood. For the funerals of Strumpshaw folk the Mayes' hired a double horse hearse from Norwich.

Another spectacle was to see new tumbrel wheels being rolled up the slope out of the yard and along the road to the forge. Here the wheel would be 'iron shod' by Herbert Colman assisted by his last recruit, Neville Burton of Lingwood. It was a rare sight, still happening in 1960, which involved heating the rim of iron in a fire on the ground. At an optimum moment the red-hot rim would be lifted by both men using tongs and lowered over the wheel, with cold water then poured over to rapidly cool red-hot metal and shrink it to make a tight fit round the wheel's circumference.

Neville Burton joined Herbert Colman in 1952. He learnt his trade at Sharman's, the Freethorpe blacksmith, shoeing horses from seven in the morning until six in the evening. He served five years before being called for service in World War II. When Herbert died in August 1975 at the age of 71 the old forge was cooled for good and Neville moved across the road where a modern version of the village smithy, Strumpshaw Engineering, was just beginning. Wesley Key, whose father had employed Herbert Mayes, had established the very kind of business which Herbert Colman knew would take over from horsepower.

With the blacksmith's forge little more than a memory the village resounded to steel being wrought. Sparks could be seen to fly as a modern type of horsepower, like powerful tractors from Italy and all manner of farm implements were serviced. When harvest came Strumpshaw Engineering was just as busy as the time when scythes needed regrinding. Combine harvesters came to have cutters replaced and high lifting trailers needed attention to 'sticky' hydraulics. In 1983 Neville Burton could be seen welding with the same care he learned at the old forge just across the road. But changes in farming economics gradually bought this operation to a close and the site became Brickfields in 1988.

Today there are horses still clip-clopping around

the village. They are much lighter and carry no more weight than a rider but they still need shoeing. It would mean a long journey to the nearest blacksmith so a farrier comes visiting, in modern transport, with readymade shoes on board, in a variety of sizes. With the aid of a portable anvil and a gas-fired forge, Philip Armes from nearby Upton comes to keep the local hoof-wear in good order. Off the shelf shoes, in a variety of styles, are given a slight adjustment to make a perfect fit.

But Strumpshaw's old forge is not totally forgotten. Many of the smith's implements were donated to the Gressenhall Museum of Rural Life and Herbert Colman Close, a housing development on the land once owned by the last blacksmith, bears testimony to Strumpshaw's industrious past.

Christine McNamara (née Colman), daughter of Herbert Colman, by the close named in his honour.

The easterly end of Strumpshaw was home to a few lighter industrialists. In the cottages behind the present post office lived Mrs Howes, the threshing contractor's wife and her two daughters, Esther and Laura. The eldest, Esther, although deaf and dumb, was a trained tailoress and earned her living as a dressmaker. Her skills enabled her to make a complete outfit for any lady in the parish getting married, right down to the under-garments.

At the junction of Norwich and Chapel Roads lived Christopher Plow. In the late 1800's he was the village cordwainer, an ancient name for shoemaker, and at one stage employed a few people in his trade.

Thomas Goffin was the local brickmaker and bricklayer. The land off Mill Road yielded good clay for brick making at the local brick kiln, just into Lingwood on the site now occupied by housing. Bricks were made locally in the days before the railways came and mechanised road transport meant bricks could be imported from large brick-makers far from Strumpshaw.

◇

Chapter 12

Tales of Two Pubs

The culture of the English pub is envied the world over and Strumpshaw has two. The Shoulder of Mutton and the Huntsman (formerly The Goat) have survived developments and legislations for more than three hundred years. With the changing fortunes of 2009, a small village supporting two pubs is unique.

The Huntsman is the historical elder. Formerly The Goat, Strumpshaw's Manor Court records show references to the house existing in 1701. It was positioned at a crossroads where the thoroughfare from Brundall to Lingwood crossed Ferrystye Way, running from Buckenham Ferry to Pack Lane and continued through the fields northwards long before the coming of the railway. In 1795 a Road Closure Order for "The Stoppage of Pack Lane" appears on a map showing The Goat and in 1804 it was well established:

'….a tenement and one acre now called The Goat, being in Strumpshaw between the way called Ferrystye Way on the East part and lands formerly of Thomas Harby on the West part and butting upon the lands formerly in the tenure of George Docking, North and upon the Common Pasture towards the South'

The Goat had been in the ownership of Francis Shepherd and later John Simonds. These days, what was once an important thoroughfare at the crossroads is merely a footpath for walkers. The track running from the top of Mill Hill is now referred to as Goat Lane.

The Goat was under the sign of St George's Brewery until 1864 when it was acquired by Youngs and Co. Under the amalgamation of Youngs Crawshay & Youngs it was held until 1958.

Some licencees had short stays and sometimes fell foul of the law. Joseph Loombe, who also combined the living with being a gardener, was accused of selling out of hours in February 1881 and Mary Ann Broom was caught permitting drunkenness in May

The Huntsman, 2007.

The Goat (now Huntsman) c1910 when beer was delivered by horse-drawn dray.

1899. In January 1901 The Goat was taken by Arthur Lake, the grandfather of Douglas Bliss who was familiar with his family's history:

'Arthur Daniel Lake was born in the end cottage near Lingwood Lodge in 1879 and grew up to become a fisherman on a Lowestoft trawler. He courted and married Sarah Ann Spooner, the eldest child of the Spooner family who kept The Shoulder of Mutton. Sarah knew from experience how to run a pub as her parents died young and she had to bring up the family as well as look after the Mutton. With the money he had saved as a fisherman, Arthur and Sarah took over The Goat and my mother, Mrs Sylvia Elvina Bliss was born there in 1901'

Four more landlords came and went. Then, in January 1920, Fred Knights arrived, or Robert Knights, as he was officially licensed. Prior to taking The Goat he was head ostler for a Norwich livery stable and was very well known to a host of horsemen. Almost every day there would be all manner of horse-drawn vehicles parked outside, as Arthur Carter recounted:

'I can remember once calling there and outside stood a hearse complete with coffin and five coaches. All the mourners were inside having a drink, which had been paid for by the deceased man. He had left strict instructions that they should call there before they

went to the church because, "I shan't be with you when you come back" he said'

In 1927 the license was taken by Alfred Brighton, another Norwich landlord who had run the city's White Lion. Son Ted, just three years old when his

Ted Brighton, a true regular at The Shoulder of Mutton, 2009.

83

Keith Sturman, Bob Rowland and Trevor Webb in Strumpshaw's gravel working, with a goat's head they unearthed in August 1972. At the time, a concocted story claimed it to be the head from The Goat (Huntsman) but it bore no comparison to the original. (PICTURE BY COURTESY OF EASTERN DAILY PRESS)

Robert Faichen at The Huntsman, 2009.

Norwich "blues man", Albert Cooper, performing at The Goat, 1982.

father took the Goat, remembers the long hours worked by his parents. Alfred was a keen bowls player and established a successful team in Strumpshaw and kept a fine bowling green at the rear of the pub. Billiards became well established with the Strumpshaw team managing to win the league shield along with 'shove halfpenny', another pub favourite in those days.

Harvest time at The Goat was particularly memorable. When the harvesters came in they would drink at the bar and leave when all their money was spent. Dudley Rowland was a neighbour of the pub for many years:

'People would say there was more beer spilled on the floor in those days than there is sold today. It was all barrels in the back, rolled up on stools. The beer used to turn up on a Wednesday for the weekend. The barrels were always rolled up and left to settle. Having been rolled along they needed time to settle, so sat there and you didn't draw anything out till the weekend'

During the summer, The Goat was often a stopping place for touring contractors from Great Yarmouth. They used vehicles called wagonettes, drawn by four smart horses, carrying twenty five passengers and it was usual to see four or five of these parked outside the pub. Arthur Carter joined them inside on many occasions:

'Each horse had a nose-bag full of food, while inside the day-trippers were consuming vast quantities of drink. At closing time, 2pm, Alfred Brighton had quite a job to get the inebriated customers to leave but it did not make too much difference, as George Hunt, the local "copper" from Cantley, had usually gone home and it was well-known that no more of him would be seen until the next day. When the people eventually got loaded, one of the party would start playing an old accordion and the drivers would get under way. Along with the clip-clop of the horse's hooves, the strains of "Nellie Dean" and "That Old Fashioned Mother of Mine" could be heard for the next ten minutes or so as the wagonettes left the village.'

The Brighton family enjoyed a record stay of fourteen years, leaving in 1941. Within living memory Ted Brighton was saddened by a decline which set in after his family departed. Amongst desperate moves to keep the trade coming The Goat attracted press interest during the license time of Frank Walpole who took over in c1967.

The stuffed head of a goat had been the feature of the bar for many years. The licensee in 1908, Mrs Newton, (John Newton 1905-11) bought a goat for half-a-crown (12.5p) from a pedlar who had called at the pub. The white goat with its twelve-inch long horns, spanning two feet and sporting a magnificent 24 inch beard was slaughtered by Harry Thompson after a year or two. Its head was mounted on a wooden shield and displayed in the bar as a talking point until 1972. In that year, a regular customer died in a road accident just days after stroking the goat's beard. Accusations of a jinx followed so the head had to go, into Langley Dyke! But apparently it returned, as these things do! The head had been touched by many regulars for more than sixty years, especially by Harry 'Buncher' Thompson, who was very handy with a poleaxe. Woe betide anyone who ever dared occupy his favourite seat in the bar.

Several landlords tried to breathe new life from behind the bar. In 1982 Dave Rowe came from Kent to take over and for the best part of a year bravely regenerated the clientele. He brought in musicians and introduced Petanque, the French game of bowls, even playing host to French players. Dave Rowe had tried his best but the pub closed in September 1983.

The Goat had always been a true 'man's pub' and one prospective landlord saw it as "a cold house". Ambitious plans to refurbish and reopen fell through so by February 1984 the house was back on the estate agent's books.

Later in 1984 an ambitious scheme produced a new pub. The Goat was gutted, along with its name and enlarged for a rebirth as The Huntsman. Then in September 1989, two ambitious landladies, Annabel Gay and Jo Hall, who had met on a hotel training course at Norwich's City College, were confident it would work as a pub and restaurant.

More landlords and a switchback ride of a survival led to receivership. In 1993 Robert Faichen came and took control and stayed for a few months until The Huntsman was taken over by Labatts. He moved up to Sheffield for a time but returned here after applying for the tenancy. Somehow he had fallen for Strumpshaw.

Robert had entered the specialist trade of taking on tenancies of pubs which had failed, just to keep them afloat, until a sale or rescue deal was implemented. He was the kind of chap who could cope with the task, born in Hong Kong of Scottish origins, and worldly travelled, he had been fascinated by the pub trade since leaving school. Before Strumpshaw his craft was honed on running thirty six pubs in two and a half years.

Two and a half years into his Strumpshaw contract

Shoulder of Mutton, c1978.

The Huntsman was acquired by Enterprise Inns. This organisation, founded in 1991, owns a few thousand houses nationwide including several close to Strumpshaw. There is a massive rent to find and Robert is committed to selling particular beers, bought at prices higher than those paid by his competitors, in a pub which is not freehold. 2009 was a tough time for Robert Faichen.

At the top of Long Lane, sharing a neighbourhood with St Peter's is the Shoulder of Mutton. "Salvation and damnation staring at each other" as some old folk have said. The Mutton has survived the years mainly through its incumbents having something on the side, a trade, as well as running the pub. It has also served in other ways. In 1854-56 it was the post office, with John Spooner the publican, appointed as postmaster.

The Shoulder demonstrates its past. The Lacons falcon, symbol of early ownership perches above the swinging sign of a free house, in turn acquired from Whitbread. In the churchyard opposite lies Edmund Salter Whitbread, Strumpshaw's rector for fifty seven years. He was the grandson of Ive, the half-brother of Samuel

The Lacon's falcon, a reminder of earlier brewers.

Whitbread who in 1742 started the famous brewery.

Most records show The Shoulder of Mutton as being here before the mid 19th century. A landlord in 1836 was James Thompson and the place was lot No 33 in a sale by Coltishall Brewery on 17 November 1841. That was the year John Spooner took over and combined it with his trade as wheelwright and carpenter, eventually passing the business to his son, also John, by then a master carpenter. During renovation work at his house in 1981, Dudley Rowland removed a wooden mantle-shelf which revealed the signature of John Spooner with the date of 1881. Craftsmen often signed their work this way.

Four more landlords followed the Spooner family before Reginald Arthur Downs arrived in February 1937. His trade was haulage contractor and coal merchant which he operated from the pub. After his departure, Edmund Percy Monkman was landlord in August 1949.

Within most of Strumpshaw's living memories Charlie and Bridget Nicholls became licensees in May 1957. The first customer to cross their new threshold was George "Sixer" Thompson, a stal-

The Shoulder of Mutton c1910.

Shoulder of Mutton. Left to right: Charlie Nichols, Bridget Nicholls, George "Sixer" Thompson and Len Cardy.

The Shoulder of Mutton Darts Team on reaching the Semi Finals of The Mercury Cup c1962. Left to right, back: Terry Atkins, Kenny Patterson. Front: Pete Matthews, John Lake, Gerry Jermy, Tony Patterson, Ted Copeman, Gerry Patterson. (PICTURE BY COURTESY OF EASTERN DAILY PRESS)

Annie Miller and Rod Brown at The Shoulder of Mutton.

wart of the village who had been christened by the Rev Whitbread. Reedham born Charlie settled comfortably into Strumpshaw's village life bringing a lifetime of experience to bear on the trade. An apprenticed engineer he saw six years war service, with three and half of those spent in the Middle East. Before the Mutton he had worked for the Eastern Electricity Board. Charlie and Halvergate born Bridget married just a week before taking charge of the Mutton.

The Shoulder of Mutton became a flourishing social centre under Charlie's landlordship. At weekends a pianist would play to accompany anyone, including Charlie, who would care to sing. A darts club of fifty members thrived, playing in local leagues and were regular competitors in the Mercury Darts Competition. Even the cribbage team played for league matches. During all this time Charlie was the school bus driver, collecting local children for their journeys to and from the schools away from the village, with fellow driver Arthur Carter. After a record thirty one years of serving their local patrons and taking a spell as parish councillor, Charlie and Bridget retired. Only the Spooner family, from 1841 to 1903, could claim a longer incumbency.

In June 1986 the licensees register added Anne Miller. Annie who came with a honed experience of having managed Haddiscoe Crown and the East Norwich Inn at Acle, took the Shoulder with Rodney Brown and "turned it round" by introducing food. Annie had trained as a cook at fifteen and as Rod put it "nobody's ever made money out of selling beer". The Shoulder of Mutton entered a new era and Annie will always remember her first impression:

'I thought it was a lovely little pub but it really was a gentleman's watering hole, in a lot of respects. I heard rather a lot of swearing going on and even I might swear when I'm angry. Many years ago my mother had bought me a china pig so I put it as a swear box on the counter and charged

people accordingly. *From the June when we moved here, towards Christmas, it was quite full and we didn't know what to do with the money. We emptied it one evening and there was £80 in it and so it paid for the first Strumpshaw Pensioners Christmas Party. Now, of course, it's grown from there'*

Annie had set the seal as all good publicans can do. Quizzes and fancy dress parties, fireworks and petanque, good food and the right company along with renovations and additions to the premises kept the Shoulder ahead of the times. Even the bad language in the bar paid dividends with the pensioner's party now a permanent fixture on Strumpshaw calendars.

Those good times were also affected by Government rulings on monopolies and mergers. Whitbread, who leased the Shoulder, were found to have too many outlets so fifty two houses in this area were then traded under the Lacons sign and were eventually bought by Adnams. Then the ultimate challenge was the Shoulder becoming a free house. During all these times Annie and Rod stayed good neighbours of St Peter's, with parking for Sunday services and glass recycling proceeds given to church funds.

The licensing statement above the door permits Anne Miller and Rod Brown to ply their trade. But they each had good reason to take a more relaxed life style and handed the reins to Jenny Blackburn and her partner Ian Stones. Annie and Rod still get behind the bar to give the hosts a break. Jenny had

Right: *Mike Turner in charge of food, garden party 2009.*

Far right: *Jenny Blackburn.*

never dreamed of running a pub but after first coming to help, 16 years ago she is doing exactly what she loves:

'I started to cook for Annie when she was ill, for a month. Five years later she never asked me to stop so I just kept on. She offered it to us and first of all we did say no. It was a mammoth thing to do but we decided to accept. We thought if we don't who else would? We started in earnest in 2007 and we're committed to keeping the pub open'

Ian Stones met Jenny on weekend visits to Norfolk through his father having a boat on the broads. Hartlepool born and a young veteran of the Iraq war, as a member of 2nd Parachute Regiment, RHA, Ian is now well adapted to Strumpshaw life:

'I came out of the army and did various things, including working for Jenny's dad. I was doing an events job with The Russell Organisation for the Adnam's trailer so I went to them and did a course on beer etc. Jenny had taken over here with Sally. Sally left and Jenny suggested I take it on and that was that'

Ian Stones at The Shoulder of Mutton, 2009.

And that really is that except to say the English pub remains the true centre of this community. How would you record its contribution for future generations? A favourite story is of Austin South who lived in St Peter's Close. When he had cause to nip to the gents, Auty, as he was affectionately known, would remove his false teeth and place them in his glass of beer, to stop anyone drinking it!

A famous visitor at The Shoulder. This showman's engine once belonged to Bostock and Wombwell, the celebrated family of travelling showmen.

◇

Chapter 13

Strumpshaw Hall; a Squire's Seat

In most English villages the hall was the seat of the squire or major landowner. Historically it was the court of justice for tenants on the estate and stemmed from the manor house. Strumpshaw's seat was established at the end of Low Town with an acreage to make it the biggest estate in the village, with two halls; old and new.

The Old Hall, dating from 1646, was built for John Stubbe who inherited the estate in 1607. The construction of flint and brick, with a central front door has later brickwork on its west while the house was substantially altered in the 18 century. The hall's owners claim to their position in Strumpshaw is proven by Mrs Stubbe who is buried in the church on the south side of the chancel where her memorial states: 'Sarah Stubbe, that devout widow who departed this life in the true faith, 6 August 1665'

In the 18th century William Springall lived in the hall until he was laid to rest in the church. A small brass marks a vault under the pew at the east end of the nave by the north wall. His large memorial plaque on the south wall of St Peter's tells everyone who enters that William Springall, Gent who died aged 65 on 3 November 1757 was: 'a sincere Christian who left this life for a better one'. Strumpshaw life was tough in those times, even for the squire.

Thomas Tuck, a "yeoman" farmer of Witton, was the hall's next occupier. He married Mary Saul and their son Charles Edward (1808-1889) was Mayor of Norwich in 1864. Another son, William Gilbert, Strumpshaw born in 1810, went to school in North Walsham, took a BA at Jesus College, Cambridge and became a rector. Most of Strumpshaw's squired families produced a man of the cloth.

The Tuck family's time in Strumpshaw was

The Old Hall, Strumpshaw.

marred by sadness and tragedy. Of their eight children, six sons and two daughters, at least three lived short lives. William died at five years in 1810 after being dragged from a horse, Mary Susana at 26 years in 1828 and Richard 25 years in 1838

Thomas Tuck died in October 1834 followed on 30 November 1835 by his wife Mary. The estate then fell to their eldest son, Thomas Gilbert Tuck who in 1825 had married Lydia Ann the first daughter of Robert Gilbert of Postwick Hall. After the death of his mother, Thomas built the new hall in 1835. The late Georgian house in white brick with its fluted Doric columns became the family home.

Thomas Gilbert Tuck was a respected member of the community. He was Deputy Lieutenant and Magistrate of the county but in 1842 he took opposition to the coming of the Yarmouth and Norwich Railway with its planned route through his Strumpshaw estate. Like many landowners, he stubbornly objected to this intrusive means of travel. But an Act of Parliament was in force along with compulsory purchase orders and a compromising land exchange so he had to tolerate the line through Strumpshaw.

Far worse for Thomas and his wife, than having to accept the railway, was the sudden death at 29 of their only child, Helen Louisa on 3 December 1856. Folklore has preserved the history of her plunge, or leap, to death from an upper window at the new hall where a stone cross commemorates. Tales handed down for more than 150 years talk of illicit love for a soldier living in the village, imprisonment in the upstairs room and burial in the orchard. In the churchyard, at the foot of her parents' tomb, a marble memorial states:

'Helen Louise, Adorned with many gifts, mental and personal, fondly loved and so deeply mourned. How hard to say Thy will be done'

The traditional respect for Helen Tuck's demise remained evident in 1960. In that year the hall was let to paying tenants after the passing of Mrs Holmes, the widow of the last squire. A newly resident family were advised not to use one particular room where the shutters were always closed.

After the passing of Helen Louise, Thomas Tuck was faced with departing this world without issue so his will of 1857 stated that he had:

'Demised all his real estate and appurtances to Lydia Anne his wife, during her life and after her decease to the use of the Revd Clement Gilbert and his assigns for life with remainder to the use of first, second and all other sons'

The New Hall during celebrations for the life of Wesley Key, 12 October 1995.

Revd Clement Gilbert was Lydia Ann's brother and rector of Hemsby since 1853. Thomas Gilbert Tuck died 27 September 1862 followed by Lydia on 15 May 1864. Revd Gilbert, then 42 years old, took up his privileged residency of Strumpshaw Hall with Agnes his wife and their three children, Cecil, Constance and Catherine. But Clement Gilbert passed away on 29 July 1876, at 54, leaving his 20 year old son, Cecil Thomas Clement Gilbert as landowner and head of the household. After five years the family moved to Aylsham and Strumpshaw Hall was prepared for a total change of ownership.

William James Owen Holmes at Emmanual College, Cambridge, 1858 (PICTURE BY COURTESY OF ST JOHN'S LIBRARY, CAMB.).

The estate was sold in two lots on 19 July 1881. Lot 1 comprising the hall, offices, gardens and shrubberies was bought by William James Owen Holmes who had been living in Lowestoft after moving from an estate in Penally, Pembrokeshire, North Wales. Holmes was returning to Norfolk where he was born, the only son of Rev William Holmes, rector of Scole and Thelveton, whose wife Jemima was a daughter of Sir Charles Flower, Bart. William J O Holmes had been educated at Harrow, finishing at Emmanuel College Cambridge in 1858. Strumpshaw was about to receive a bit of established squirearchy

The Holmes' had celebrated the birth of their only son, William Charles Flower in North Wales. He was one year old at the time of the Strumpshaw purchase. Life had been grand at Penally House, attended by six servants, which included Edward Moyse from Scole who had accompanied the family to Pembrokeshire. In 1881, the year of the move to Strumpshaw, William J O was elected a Fellow of the Linnean Society, the world's oldest active organisation devoted exclusively to natural history.

Holmes found Strumpshaw a place of beauty. The fen with its scenery and variety of birds, persuaded him to chose the property at the time when conservation was a little used word in the English language. Once he was settled there was so much to see, shoot and stuff. Then there was the added distinction of being able to mark and claim the swans which graced the River Yare

The swan mark of William Holmes, 1882.

where it flowed by the estate.

The responsibility to manage the Strumpshaw territory would eventually fall to the young Holmes. In 1897 he was dispatched to the Royal College of Agriculture at Cirencester, to learn the business of running his father's estate. He settled into his year at the age of 17, looking young among his contemporaries, a squire in the making. But young William had a mind of his own. The agricultural college may have been the first of its kind in the English speaking world but it was near to the railway works at Swindon and these were closer to the heart of young Holmes. First he stole away at every opportunity then courses in engineering led ultimately to him becoming an engine driver on the Great Western Railway. He was very happy but eventually had to come home to Strumpshaw.

At home, his father enjoyed life as a sporting fisherman and the agriculture on the estate. He loved the trees in the park and as such refused to have cattle grazing there, fearing they would damage the bark. He took no part in politics or local affairs although he was present at the instigation of the parish council in 1894 and he sat on the Blofield Bench of Justices.

William Holmes took his place in the community. At church on Sunday, the congregation had to be in and seated before the Holmes' arrived and then stand as they made their way to the front. Ellen Holmes in her silk gown and William with his walking stick were accompanied by a maid as they took their pew, just one from the front. These were the footsteps to be followed by their son.

Squire Holmes was well-known to the fraternity of Broadland wildfowlers. One of their characters, Archie Gibbs, would sit and regale in his favourite haunt, just over the river at Coldham Hall, the inn for anglers and fowlers:

'One day I ketched a rare old termagant in a trap, what I'd set for a woodcock on Strumpshaw Marsh. I went along arly in the morning and no sooner did I get near the trap than my old dog

William Charles Flower Holmes, centre in back row, at Royal Agricultural College, 1897.

William Holmes, standing by engine, fifth from left, during his time at Swindon.

started growlin. Suffin bounced up by the trap, a rare big old bird, flapped his wings at me and snapped his beak. He looked as big as an eagle. I took him up to old Squire Holmes at Strumpshaw Hall and we put it alive into a hen coop. He give me a quid for it. That was fifty years ago when a quid was real money. What do you think that were? A marsh harrier! The old squire had a rare lot of stuffed birds up at the hall'

Mabel and William Holmes with daughter Ellen Mary c1919.

William James Owen Holmes died on 11 September 1908. His funeral service was held at Scole parish church on 18 September where his body was laid to rest in the family vault. William Charles Flower Holmes, the son, was now shouldering the responsibility for which he had apparently been trained. The all important man in the community needed a wife so

he was matched to Mabel Barnes, the youngest daughter of Edward and Ann Barnes of The Hollies.

The wedding took place at St Margaret's Church, Lowestoft on 30 September 1913 with a few relatives and friends present. The new couple set up home at Scarborough but eventually returned to Strumpshaw to live with William's widowed mother in the Hall. In 1914 their first child, Ellen Mary Flower Holmes was born and more than sixty years on, 'Mary', as she became known, recounted the whole story:

'I was born at The Hollies. My granny wouldn't have me down at the other place because there wasn't room! People find that amusing but I stayed there till I was five. My mother and father had a house at Scarborough but income got less and less so the sensible thing was to move back to the family home with granny. But my mother and granny never got on. I preferred to be at my aunt's house, The Hollies, because it was a bit more cheerful. Down there (at the hall) my father's mother's old companion was still alive and oh, that was eerie. Perhaps you won't believe this but there was poverty. Things were getting less and less. However poor, you always had maids. We only had three and I was always being told of the time when there were five and we had a coachman who would have had people under him. We had only two gardeners when there had been four so you see all the time I was hearing how poor we were. Then my granny died and I moved down'

Mary's father was anti social, she felt, and would rather be associating with the "black sheep" of the

The Hollies at the time of Ellen Mary Holmes' birth.

parish. Always in tow was "Guymer, the old family retainer", a useful chap who looked after young Mary's goat and built it a cart, as goat-carts were novel in those days.

From 1897-1901 a member of the "old retainer's" family was employed at the hall, as a maid servant. She was Emma Louise Guymer, born at Leamington in 1882, where her mother was a domestic servant. Emma came to Strumpshaw and lived with her aunt and uncle, Emma and Walter Alexander. South Walsham born Walter was Strumpshaw's wheelwright, carpenter and clerk on the new parish council.

During this time, 19 year old Emma became pregnant. In due course she gave birth to a daughter, Helen Polly Guymer on 20 April 1901 but was dispatched to Birmingham and in 1906 married William Latimer Symonds in neighbouring Edgbaston. Baby Helen stayed in Strumpshaw to be raised by her grandparents, Walter and Emma Alexander.

For a lifetime the family guarded the secret that squire Holmes 19 year old son was the father of Helen. In 1967 two ladies from Birmingham visited Strumpshaw on a pilgrimage into this period of history and met Christine Colman who was then living in the house once occupied by Helen's grandparents. Helen Polly Guymer died in 1986.

Despite having to harbour Strumpshaw's 'fleshly sins' Mrs Holmes was a charitable lady. She was forever aware of the burdens brought on any family when a baby arrived and Alice Manthorpe, Strumpshaw's post-woman, was always first with the news:

'When there was a baby coming along, old lady Holmes would inquire of the parents how they were fitted out for clothes for the child. There were laundered clothes ready and she used to loan them to these people for so many weeks and then they'd got to hand them back in. After use, the clothes would be sent back, to the laundry, ready for the next one on the list. Then they had a club. People would pay a penny or two a week and she would add so much to that and when it was distributed they would go to Bonds in Norwich and buy what they wanted'

"Old lady Holmes" died in November 1917 and so made way for the new squire and his wife. But Mary, as the young Ellen was now better known, soon discovered there were concerns in her father's home and there was talk of poverty. Her mother was always out and about and would entertain with endless tea parties. To keep domestic life running smooth William made a metal disc, slightly larger than an old penny, red one side and white the other, to hang by the back door. If Mable was entertaining her friends the maid would display the red side to advise William against entering the house: when it was white he could come in.

If the squire's home was feeling the pinch of poverty it was certainly shared just down the road in Low Town. William Pulford and his family had always recounted his time of working on the estate and surviving the winter on a barrel of dried herring and potatoes. They were allowed skimmed milk and the used 'second-hand' tea leaves from the teapot at the hall.

William Holmes at the controls of SS Flower, his steam yacht, which he plied from Strumpshaw Fen, c1916.

William Holmes may not have become the perfect squire but he was never idle. In a small workshop on the estate he built a generator and was making electricity when few people in the village knew of the invention. His other passion was steam so he became the owner of a steam launch aptly named the SS Flower. Nothing pleased William more than to welcome wife Mabel and her friends aboard, dressed in their finery for an afternoon's cruise. He would then open the throttle and shower them in steam and smuts.

From March 1918 Billy Cowles, whose father and mother came to Strumpshaw as railway gate-keepers on the hall estate, was employed as "boot and garden boy" for squire Holmes:

William Holmes with daughter Ellen Mary c1922.

would visit the Shoulder of Mutton with George Guymer, the old family retainer, for drinks all round with his group getting 'as tight as newts' A highlight of William's leisurely rounds was his group of hand-bell ringers, led by himself and always ready to entertain.

Mary Holmes considered, sixty years later, that her childhood had been peculiar. She could never, understand why her father was not earning a living. He was always ill and used to get terribly depressed. Above everything, Mary felt she was a disappointment having not been born a boy. Her only happy escape in life was to go down to the Old Hall Farm tenanted by Harry Oliver from 1914:

'A typical squire, he had I suppose six pairs of hobnailed and ordinary boots and a pair of thigh boots in black leather. Every so often he had the craze: these boots had to be greased. He'd come round and say "I want my boots doing Bill, you'll find them all in the gun room", and mind you, I had a boot cleaning place of my own for boots and knives, so I used to go in the gun room and do them. He came in once and left me half a bottle of port wine and said, "You can have a drink when you're doing them, and a few favours of course". He was as good as gold, a proper gentleman'

Young Holmes loved the people of Strumpshaw and proved a total break from the traditional squire. He

William Holmes, seated centre, with his group of Strumpshaw hand-bell ringers, in front of the New Hall, c1910.

'I spent all my young life with this Mr Oliver, whenever I could escape. He had some peculiar gift: a power over animals. He had curious grey eyes with very dark lines round the pupils. They could be so kind but my goodness they could be so hard. When I was about eight, he used to sell various horses, riding horses and shire horses, and he'd put me on to ride them to show how quiet they were but they were anything but quiet. He had a sort of box cart and for a special treat I was allowed to sit on the back of the cart and hold this horse.'

Mabel Holmes had hoped to reform William but daughter Mary maintained it was wishful thinking. Her mother had come from such a pious background: the Barnes had lived with the church as the hub of the village and Mary had been told by her father never to say the Lord's Prayer. As a result life at home was a succession of explosions. Time proved that William was finding a solace in alcohol and suffering from diabetes. Billy Cowles had to bear the brunt of keeping his master happy and recalled the times when William was the only person living in the hall:

'They had a good cellar up there then and I've seen him have two bottles of port wine before five in the morning. I used to bring it down to the old hut in the bottom of the garden. As soon as I'd seen it lit up in the morning, at six o'clock you'd know he'd started on the bottle and he'd be roughly on that for nearly a fortnight. Then the doctor would have him put in bed for a week. He'd get up and be a proper gentleman for a week then off on the bottle again'

William Charles Flower Holmes died after a short illness on 7 March 1924 at the age of 45. His diabetes never benefitted from the new production method for insulin which had come in 1923. William's last will and testament demonstrated his concern for the people whose company he had come to enjoy. There was £25 to George Guymer, "the old family retainer" and £10 to each labourer at Strumpshaw Hall of four year's service if either he or his mother were residing there. He left £500 to the rector and churchwardens of Strumpshaw, in trust for investment, so the income could be used to supply coal each winter for the needy of the parish. Above all, a settlement made within days of his marriage to Mabel Barnes secured her in widowhood.

The last squire was gone and his only child was a ten year old girl, Mary Holmes. Mabel, her widowed mother, still had family close by as her two sisters Anne and Catherine lived at The Hollies. The Barnes' girls were the residue of the squirearchical system and young Mary was the last witness to a lifestyle and social round which was running out of time.

Mary's maternal grandfather Edward Barnes had died in 1898 followed by grandmother Mary in 1914. Frederick Robert Whitbread, solicitor and surviving trustee, then sold The Hollies to the second daughter, Anne Harriet Barnes, in February 1915. Eldest Mary Kate and third girl Catherine were not mentioned in the deal. Anne and Catherine were well remembered for the difficult times at The Hollies as Hilda Rowland recalled:

'The two Miss Barnes' lived in The Hollies and they never spoke to each other. Talk about going to church to worship God. They never walked to church together and they never walked home together. Their sister, Mable Holmes would come along too. She'd walk down the church and go in the pew. Nobody else was allowed to sit in their pew. Annie, she was a nice little one. Friendly; if you met her on the road she'd always say 'Hello' to you but not Kate (Catherine), the other one'

Catherine, known latterly as Kate, devoted much of her life to being a British Red Cross nurse. She tended recuperating soldiers returning wounded from the first war and entertained a whole detachment of the military in the gardens at the Hollies. She was presented to Princess Alexander during an award ceremony at Sandringham.

A regular visitor to The Hollies was Frederick Whitbread. He was the youngest son of Strumpshaw's famous rector and lived at Tottenhill with his housekeeper, Harriet Giles. At Strumpshaw, the fastidious Frederick came to advise Anne Barnes on her business affairs and at breakfast feasted on the best parts of six boiled eggs. He loved the wine from The Hollies cellar and ate grapes while "spitting the pips everywhere" all of which amused the young Mary Holmes. She later learned that unmarried Frederick Whitbread was the father of an illegitimate daughter.

On 13 May 1922 Frederick Whitbread died suddenly at his Tottenhill residence. His funeral and interment took place at Strumpshaw on 18 May where his body was laid to rest in the family plot "in a brick-built grave", the work of John Gedge of Blofield. The chief mourners were his brother William and Mrs Giles.

The Whitbread family grave had been planned

Enjoying the sea at Walcot. Mary and mother c1918.

Catherine Barnes, extreme right, as a Red Cross nurse to wounded soldiers from first war c1916.

The Whitbread family graves in Strumpshaw churchyard.

and was already the resting place of Frederick's parents and his two sisters with space allotted for William. William died in September 1925 and completed the family plot. The railed graves of the Whitbread family received little attention until 1936, after the death of Harriet Giles. In her will of 1934 she stipulated to her trustees a sum of money to be used for the upkeep of her parent's and daughter's graves in Swardeston churchyard. She also included the resting place of the late Frederick Robert Whitbread in Strumpshaw churchyard and Mary Holmes knew why.

The Barnes' reign was also drawing to a close. Anne Harriet died in a nursing home during June 1938 having suffered a stroke while enjoying an after-noon visit to her favourite cinema in Prince of Wales Road, Norwich. The Hollies had already been sold in 1935 and Catherine had gone to live in Brundall.

The Hollies had been with the Barnes Family for more than one hundred years. A subsequent owner sold off much of the land and divided the main home from its domestic quarters which was taken up by Paul and Shelia Ashford in April 1958:

'We had been in the house, Holly Lodge, for only a few days when I had a visitation from Miss Kate (Catherine) Barnes. She had walked here from her home in The Uplands, Brundall and I had the distinct impression that I was being inspected and also required to provide tea and thinly sliced cucumber sandwiches. She then gave me a fascinating insight into a more feudal way of Strumpshaw life'

That feudal way of life had taken quite a turning in 1925. After the last squire passed on Mrs Holmes engaged Albert Key, an enterprising farmer from Beighton to tenant the Old Hall Farm and manage the estate. The sole heir to the Strumpshaw property was a 12 year old girl, Ellen Mary, the last squire's daughter. Albert Key integrated into Strumpshaw's community and living on the edge of the hall estate was a young Clive Jermy:

'Old Albert Key was a character all the children recognised in his pony and trap. With friends, I was chestnut collecting in the hall grounds and he caught us. He took my bag of nuts and as we were leaving, he appeared again and called us back saying that his wife said he should let us take them! I was collecting rabbit food one day, in his clover field and he stopped his pony and shouted at me to stop. In defence, I said that my uncle did it! The next thing I heard was that our local bobby had called on my uncle! Albert Key was a man to watch. He wasn't the squire but the next in line. If I could meet him as an adult I expect he was charming and indeed a lovable man'

For the sake of a few chestnuts and some rabbit food Albert Key had encountered the future Dr Clive Jermy, a leading authority on ferns and mosses!

Strumpshaw Hall was home to the widowed Mabel Holmes until she died in 1960. Her father-in-law's hunting ground became well known in wild-fowling circles and was admired by James Wentworth Day (1899-1983), the well-published writer and broadcaster. Sixty years ago he described sailing passed Strumpshaw Fen:

'The wide horizons of the marshlands opened up. On the left lay the Strumpshaw Marshes, rough and reedy. On their broad, dyke-seamed levels, herds of red poll and Friesian cattle moved slowly, munching at the marsh vegetation. Beyond, stood tall and shaggy woods, old and beautiful. Somewhere behind them lay the old hall of Strumpshaw where dwelt that fine old Broadland squire and great naturalist, the late Squire Holmes. Old-fashioned woods of oak and ash and elm where the pheasants feed and crow, and woodcock sit crouched in the ferns. And then the marshes with their broad reedy dykes, their pulk-holes like miniature broads where teal whistle under the moon, and water rails squeal like small pigs. A good old squire's old-fashioned estate, part of the very back-cloth and back-bone of rural England'

Chapter 14

◇

Strumpshaw Fen: a Reserved Occupation

When William Holmes bought the Strumpshaw Hall estate in 1881 he arrived with trophies. He adorned the walls of Strumpshaw Hall with spoonbills, golden eagles, deer heads and various other stuffed specimens from his previous estate in Wales. Conservation was a rare word in the English language when William Holmes took to shooting across the fen.

The Broad at Strumpshaw Fen, 2007.

The Fen was part of the estate. Bounded by the River Yare there was 300 acres of marshland with grazing, the silted remains of a broad with boat access to the river, numerous dykes, carrs, reed-beds; the source of Strumpshaw's traditional roofing material and a rich variety of wildlife. Maps show the broad evident in 1846 but partially visible when Holmes came in 1881. During the 1920's the Stone family with their young daughter Ruby moved into the vicinity of the fen:

'We lived in an old farmhouse along the road to the broad. I became friendly with a girl by the name of Lena Markham, who lived with her parents in the house adjoining Strumpshaw Broad. Her father was a gamekeeper on the Strumpshaw Hall Estate. Lena owned a small rowing boat and on special occasions she used to take me rowing and we would explore this small waterway, which, even in those days was fairly

overgrown with reeds. Nevertheless, she was a capable person and we spent many happy hours on the broad. I remember Lena showing me a black line which had been painted on the boat shed, and this she said was how far the water rose in the 1912 flood'

The great flood of 1912 devastated Norfolk one day in August, when nine inches of rain fell in twenty four hours. The fen was under water and sustained considerable damage. Much of it had previously been grazing ground for cattle which is now evident with surviving posts, where gates gave access to different areas. Maps show drainage wind-pumps existed before 1912 but many are known to have been swept away and never replaced.

William Holmes died in 1908 and the estate was inherited by his son. But William junior's interests led other ways and the fen more or less went the way of nature. He in turn passed on in 1924 and the estate was managed by a tenant farmer. Nature continued its course so much that the fen was eventually given an SSSI, Site of Special Scientific Interest.

A turning point for the neglected fen came in 1966 with the arrival in Strumpshaw of Dr Martin George. Having been promoted to Regional Manager of

Dr Martin George, 2009.

Mud pumpers take a breather.

The broad begins to clear.

Mike Blackburn, 2009.

Mudcat fun on Strumpshaw Fen.

Nature Conservancy, Martin George moved with his family into Bellvue House in Tinker's Lane. It provided a grandstand view of the fen but they soon changed the name to Marsh View. But the fen did need managing so Dr George would set off with a bow saw and tackle scrub clearance:

"I used to go down and help the reed-cutters. Wesley Key was the owner so with his permission I did a certain amount of work, but I was one person and there were 300 acres. Wesley asked if I'd like to hire it but I knew I couldn't possibly afford it. I told him that I knew an organisation who might well be interested because I knew the RSPB had been looking for a reserve in the Broads for years. That's how it came to be the RSPB reserve"

A lease was signed and an RSPB dream had been realised. A tremendous amount of work lay ahead if Strumpshaw Fen was to become a reserve so a warden was found by the name of Mike Blackburn. Born in Chester, his entry into the world of conservation came from working with Shell Research and Marketing, developing a water weed killer. He graduated to nature reserves and worked at six sites before starting in Strumpshaw on 6 June 1975. Mike's "D-Day" presented him with 310 acres of potential development, accompanied by major problems. He was given a year for surveying and planning: without a budget for management:

'I had reed-fen, a broad and areas open to the River Yare, nutrient polluted by Whitlingham Sewerage Works outfall. In dry periods 25% of the river flow was sewage outfall, hence weedless waterways, very poor reed and all dominated by nutrient loving vegetation like reed sweet grass, hairy willow herb and reed canary grass. 50% of the fen had been taken over by scrub. The meadows had been neglected of grazing or haying for many years so were covered in 4ft high vegetation. There was woodland with the best bits just clear, having been felled previously and the rest of alder. Nevertheless, surveying showed potential for a wide variety of waterways with meadow birds, plants, invertebrates, amphibians, reptiles and mammals.

This latest reserve was launched in June 1976. By then the RSPB was more than halfway to its £1 million appeal to buy land for new sites and Strumpshaw added to the county's other reserves at Snettisham, Titchwell and Wolferton.

The general public was still a year away from being able to walk freely at Strumpshaw Fen. The broad, whilst on the maps of 1846 had disappeared but was set to return by a major operation, implemented by Mike Blackburn and his staff:

'Dams and embankments began in 1978 and following the Broad Dyke dam's construction, with the broad being mud-pumped by "mudcats" in 1983. It was in essence a giant vacuum cleaner, sucking up the mud and depositing it in a holding area, to allow the water to run back. Floating "hover" vegetation was managed by mowing which in turn provided food for various species of wildfowl.

In the early 1980's government policy gave us Employment Training, enabling recruitment of high quality wardening staff via the Guardian noticeboard. I had two wardens and a 15-strong team. This allowed a huge push forward in every aspect of management planning including provision of visitor route-ways and other facilities. We achieved, high, unpolluted, controlled water levels, increased reed quality, reduced scrub re-invasion (much was cleared previously), and severely reduced nutrient-loving vegetation. Reed-cutting was scaled down and finally done by reserve staff only. The result was a huge increase in all reed-fen birds, like reed warblers, and more importantly, the bearded tit. Milk parsley population swelled, hugely resulting in the swallow-tail population going from just three records in 1975 to 45 adults in one day in 1993. Marsh harriers began breeding in 1980 and have bred every year since, in increasing numbers.

I pursued a very active land acquisition policy and the basic 310 acres was enlarged to 2000 by acquisition of fen to the Brundall Boatyards, Buckenham and Cantley Marshes, Surlingham and Rockland Marshes. As a result of this and the management carried out, the site achieved National Nature Reserve Status in 1996.

Buckenham and Cantley Marshes were acquired in order to safeguard the site for Englands only Bean Goose flock and up to 10,000 Wigeon and is now important for White Footed Geese too. Improved water tables have increased the importance of the site for breeding lapwing, redshank, snipe and avocet too.

Visiting, although very restricted to begin with, became possible and busy later; 20,000 per year peak, as the dams and embankments allowed access across the reed-fen and wet-ways. A number of hides were gradually sited around the reserve for visitor's enjoyment. It became busier when a schools educational facility was set up and run very professionally, by Beryl Ogden, on an almost daily basis, through the 1980's and early 1990's'

Celebrity ornithologist, Bill Oddie (centre, hand on binoculars) at RSPB Strumpshaw Fen for the launch of a special weekend, August 1987. (PICTURE BY COURTESY OF EASTERN DAILY PRESS)

In 2009 the welcoming sight of the broad betrays nothing of its reclamation, 26 years ago. Watching the fen's development as part of a lifetime devoted to nature conservation, Dr Martin George, in retirement, still finds it a wonderful place to live. Testimony to his foresight is to see Tinker's Lane thronging with bird-watchers while correspondents publish their Strumpshaw sightings on the World Wide Webb. The work continues with current warden, Tim Strudwick:

'Strumpshaw now extends over 188 hectares (457 acres), of which 125 ha (305 acres) are leased from Strumpshaw Hall. Encouraging more people to enjoy the reserve, without damaging the sense of peace and tranquillity that people find here, will be a delicate balancing act. Even with a few more visitors, Strumpshaw Fen will provide a more peaceful alternative to the RSPB's busiest reserves.

The restoration continues. Clearance of trees and scrub has progressed, and between 1995 and 2001, about 4000m of ditches were reshaped and 10 hectares of fen were scraped to provide wetter reedbed. These two projects were aimed at bringing back nesting bitterns, which was successful with a booming male bittern arriving in 2002, and nesting successfully in 2004. In 2009 there were 3 male bitterns.

Marsh harriers, which first returned to the site in

1980, have increased to 5 pairs in 2009. Bearded tits have increased to around 25 pairs. Hobbies, a small dragonfly-hunting falcon, now breed regularly, little egrets (a great rarity in the UK 20 years ago) are seen daily and breed locally, and rarities like spotted crake and Savi's warbler have nested.

Other wildlife is thriving. Otters have made a remarkable recovery from near extinction in Eastern England in the 1960s. Though largely active at night, they are now seen regularly on the Broad. A less welcome arrival was American mink which colonised the site in the late 1990s. Mink devastated the local water vole population and killed large numbers of moorhens and coots. A concerted and still ongoing trapping campaign at the reserve and

Tim Strudwick.

by neighbouring landowners has now removed most of the mink, and allowed the water voles to recover.

But not all is well. The continued recovery of this special corner of Broadland is under threat from the sea. Surge tides in 2006 and 2007 pushed saltwater up the River Yare and into the fen. On both occasions this caused massive fish kill, and it was several months before most of the saltwater had been flushed out by pumping. The lack of fish resulted in fewer sightings of kingfishers, and little chance of bitterns breeding successfully.

The impact on the plant life and invertebrates is less clear, though the majority of the white water-lilies had died by summer 2008. If saltwater gets into the peat, the fen flora, along with the swallowtails and other insect life will disappear. With sea level rise, we now expect such flood events to become more frequent, so to protect the fen and its wildlife, some major work is planned. New pipes will be installed to ensure the saline floodwater can flow off as soon as the river level drops, and the feasibility of diverting water from the Lackford Run into the fen to flush out the remaining salt is being investigated. These works will not keep the saltwater out, but will at least lessen the impact.

If the threat from saline floodwater can be abated, the future is bright at Strumpshaw Fen, and we can look forward to more lost species, such as ospreys returning, and more newcomers: little egrets may already be nesting, and great white egrets, spoonbills and purple herons may follow'

William Holmes' acquisition of Strumpshaw Fen enabled the realisation of a conservational dream. Ironically, he came to Strumpshaw from Pembrokeshire, the very place where Dr Martin George took his first job after university, and found a wife:

'I applied for this job teaching marine biology and I hardly new a topshell from a winkle in those days. When I arrived there was this girl who was the field assistant. She was paid £250 and I got £500 plus board and lodgings, so it wasn't too bad. We looked at one another and that was Barbara and we've been together ever since. We married in 1959 and have lived happily together ever after. She's a geographer and just as keen on natural history as I am; a good combination, so I feel a very fortunate individual.'

Martin George witnessed Strumpshaw Fen's transformation.

◇

Chapter 15

Waiting for Trains

Strumpshaw is uniquely bounded by a railway on both sides of the village. When the first train came through in 1844 most of industrial England was linked by railways. The line on the south of the village had been laid by the Norwich to Great Yarmouth Railway Company whose chairman was George Stephenson with his son Robert as chief engineer. It was Norfolk's first railway and the Parliamentary Bill to construct the route received Royal Assent on 18 June 1842.

The line's contractor, Grissel & Peto cast their price of £10,000 per mile. The route from Norwich's Thorpe Station was made difficult by objectors, as with most railway schemes at this time, when some landowners refused to allow the tracks across their estates. Through Brundall, the opposers had successfully forced the line to be laid on low ground, out of sight, along the river valley. Then came Strumpshaw's Thomas Tuck who tried to stop the railway from coming through his estate, but an act of Parliament was in force. He would get paid for the land used, so with some compromise and exchange of ground, the work got underway.

The laying of the single line started at Postwick on 20 April 1843. At Strumpshaw, two level crossings with gatekeeper's cottages were built, one to service the staithe and broad and the other where the road for Buckenham Ferry had been crossed. The nearest station for Strumpshaw was built close to the village of Buckenham Ferry, abbreviated these days to Buckenham. It was a small parish of less than a thousand acres with a population of 49. But it would prove useful for the estate it passed through, that of Sir Thomas Proctor Beauchamp, Bart and served Strumpshaw, a good walk of a mile and three quarters up Ferrystye Way.

The formal opening of the completed line was performed on 30 April 1844. Two hundred guests travelled from Norwich to Great Yarmouth in 55 minutes and enjoyed the quicker return journey of 44 minutes. The occasion was celebrated in style with a brass band playing in the open seat-less third-class carriage to entertain the passengers.

The following day the line was opened to the public with four trains each way and 1,015 passengers paid to take the ride. The fares were 3/6 first class, 2/6 second class and 1/3 third class, while cheap day returns could be bought for 5s, 4s and 2s.

The line was a single operation with an electric telegraph system controlling the trains. The principle was to prevent two trains on the line at any time but on 10 September 1874 a human error led to disaster. A mail train, which had passed through Strumpshaw was inadvertently allowed to leave Brundall while the express from London left Thorpe Station. The result was a terrible head-on collision near Thorpe Gardens at 9-45pm. The drivers, firemen, guard and 18 passengers were killed. Seventy three were trapped in the wreckage and suffered horrible injuries resulting in seven more deaths later. Such was the eventual impact of the news it was reported in the New York Times.

Following the tragedy, modern semaphore signalling was quickly introduced and the line was doubled through to Reedham in 1866. Despite the accident, the railway had proved to be a revolution. People no longer relied on horse-drawn transport or the twice daily steam packet on the river Yare, plying the Norwich to Yarmouth journey. Even at 122 miles distant, London was now within convenient reach.

The growth of traffic was such that the building of a relief line was promoted. This branched off at Brundall through Strumpshaw, with stations at Lingwood and Acle and then to Great Yarmouth's Vauxhall Station, a saving of two miles. The powers to construct the line were sought in 1878. The work involved the parishes of Brundall, Braydeston, Strumpshaw, Lingwood, Burlingham, Beighton, Acle, Tunstall, Cantley, South Walsham, Mautby and Runham. In Strumpshaw the cuttings parted the fields of Thomas Atkins but he raised no objection provided the railway company bridged his roadways. Thomas Atkins even coped with the fear of cereal crops being ignited by sparks from the passing

Billy Cowles time at Brundall Station. Back row, left to right: Bob Henry, Arthur Wright, Sid Brigham, Billy Cowles, Cecil Curtis, Len Tuck. Seated, left to right: S Haugh, Mr Rowby, Steve Rowby.

trains. When corn was sown he left an uncropped verge along the edge of the fields where the crops came close to the lines.

Most of the railway's construction came through hard physical labour and without machinery; the tools were picks, shovels and wheelbarrows. Working on the relief line were out of season fishermen from Great Yarmouth's herring fleets. They wore high leather boots and blue wool 'geansaidh' (pronounced gansy) earning them the title of the "boot and gansys".

Strumpshaw's George "Sixer" Thompson used to recount a story of how the navvies, working on the line, bricked-up a few bottles of beer during the construction of the Hemblington Road bridge. At the crossing of Ferrystye Way, the roadway which came from far away at Buckenham Ferry, a gated crossing was installed with a keeper's cottage. What then was an important thoroughfare, wide enough for horse-drawn wagons, is now a country footpath used by ramblers. The level crossing was decommissioned by the railway operators in 1961.

Some men who came to lay the line, stayed forever, like Richard Peart, a ganger who became "the highest paid man at Lingwood Station". Numbers of platelayers came to live locally, at least three of whom were elected members of Strumpshaw

Parish Council in 1897. The platelayers constantly inspected the railway line with all its component parts and generally kept watch for wear and tear.

The new line was opened in two sections. The first, from Great Yarmouth Vauxhall to Acle Station was 12 March 1883 while the rest of the stretch to Brundall was still under construction. This second section was completed and ready for inspection by 31 May 1883. The Government Inspector passed the line

Terry Atkins, whose great grandfather Thomas had no objection to the railway coming through his Strumpshaw farmlands.

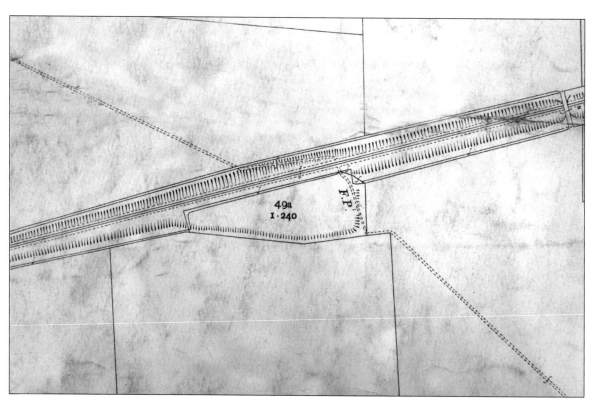

The borrow pit used during construction of the railway in 1881, now a mature woodland and skirted by the foot-path to Braydeston Church.

Above: *Sheila Ling and her celebrated collection of garden gnomes which she started collecting c1970.*

Left: *Sheila Ling in 2009, Strumpshaw's former gate-keeper.*

as fit for use and the first train to travel on the new route left Thorpe Station at 8.20am on 1 June, arriving in Great Yarmouth at 9 o'clock.

The railway left Strumpshaw a conservation legacy. What today is called Railway Wood, 1.2 acres of a semi natural woodland by the side of the line across the fields from Long lane, was the site of a 'borrow pit'. As the lines's construction progressed in 1881, earth was needed for an embankment at Braydeston so an area was purchased close by the path of the track to extract what was necessary. After the opening of the line, nature took over and today's woodland began to appear. In the summer of 2000 the site was acquired by the Blofield and District Conservation Group although they had managed it since 1994.

The taking over of nature brought an unwanted problem. Rabbits, breeding like they do, proliferated in the wood and burrowed into the sandy embankments, causing landslides along the line. For years they were controlled by Fred Stone, a railway company employee, who plied his craft of snaring the unwelcome creatures.

The Norwich and Yarmouth Railway, which first appeared on the other side of the village in 1844, was taken on by the Great Eastern Railway in 1862. This became incorporated into the London North Eastern Railway in 1923.

An unprecedented highlight occurred in May 1926 during the General Strike. This massive withdrawal of labour throughout the country came in support of the coal miners' strike and caused chaos. Among the incensed non-labouring classes were men who had always dreamed of driving a steam locomotive so a man from Acle seized the chance. With a group of others he went to Thorpe Station and took a train and drove it along the relief line through Strumpshaw, having organised the level crossings to be open. On the return journey the gates were closed and the train arrived back with a pile of gates on the front.

The relief line through Strumpshaw survived the changing times of rail operation; the end of steam and the arrival of diesel. But the semaphore signals are still illuminated by oil lamps and the upgrading to modern jointless track happened recently, in 2007, when the railway was closed for a sixteen week period. The line is a single track operation with a passing loop at Acle Station.

In 2009 at the southern end of the village the line to Lowestoft is busy but not as brisk as fifty years ago. The gates at the crossing are closed to road users but can be opened on request. These days just a few residents cross the line along with farming and delivery traffic and occasional fishermen. In 1950 Sheila Ling and her husband took the job of manning the gates because they needed somewhere to live:

The crossing on the Norwich to Lowestoft line with its manually operated gates.

'I learnt the bells, the rules and regulations all of a night, went up to Norwich for the exam and passed. The cottage was just a shell, a shack, no telephone, just one signal and the bells. The trains ran all through the night in those days but we soon got used to them. It was a twenty four hour job. No time off in those days. People just came and knocked on the door. I'd have to get out of bed many a time so I'd hang the trousers on the door and have the keys ready. People just had to wait till I got out. The first few years was mainly cattle, horses and carts, pony traps and fishermen. Cattle took their time to get across. They used to bring them over in the mornings and back again for milking, back in the afternoon and again for milking.

There were steam trains, freight trains carrying sugar beet pulp and coal to Cantley Factory. You didn't really sleep properly, I suppose no more than a couple of hours a night. There was no time when it could be closed. We'd get the bell when the train was leaving Reedham for Norwich, then Cantley and Buckenham. They told me when it was entering a section then I'd get the bell when it was clear. First it was BR, then Railtrack and now Network Rail. I did it for fifty years. When I retired I just had a letter. I was just a number'

Hard on Sheila's heels in 2009, was Steve Coman with forty year's service. He was one of three relief gate-keepers working shifts of eight hours each. In a wiser and more sophisticated age today's gate-keepers have a computer and fax machine, although the bells still ring in their 'home from home', a modular accommodation unit, plonked by the railway line. The trains thunder by in both directions, stopping at Buckenham Station if requested, while the gates at Strumpshaw are opened and closed constantly.

In 2006 the Strategic Rail Authority's figures pointed Buckenham as one of the least used stations in the country. There is little point in stopping because much of the village was razed to the ground to increase acreage by the pioneering Dutch Sugar Company when nearby Cantley factory was built in 1912. By 1954, British Railways were promoting the need to close the station and wrote to Strumpshaw Parish Council with the proposal. But opposition was fierce and a large public gathering protested firmly against the move.

At present just a few trains can stop at Buckenham Station by request, on Saturday and Sunday, a service kept primarily to serve Strumpshaw Fen. The signal box and sidings have long gone, the level crossing gates are for key-holders only and the adult population numbers 42 in just 21 houses.

Steve Coman, relief gate-keeper in 2009.

Chapter 16

Think of Steam; Think of Strumpshaw

Every May bank holiday most roads for steam enthusiasts lead to Strumpshaw. This annual assembly for steam preservationists, held in the park of Strumpshaw Hall, was started in 1968 by resident Wesley Key (1914-95). The three day event fits snugly into the parish setting where steam was once the means of agricultural mechanisation and a permanent museum was established.

Wesley Key had lived with steam all his life. His father owned engines at Grange Farm Beighton, where Wesley was born and he was fascinated by the various contractors who plied their steam trades around Strumpshaw:

Albert Key's steam engine driving a saw bench c1925.

'We had steam engines on the farm before I was born. We bought a new one in 1921. I can remember it coming home. But we didn't use it for four years because the old man who used to drive our engines was a dirty old bee and father said when he retires we'll use it. That cost us a thousand pounds. That was a lot of money; of course things were beginning to get better then after the 1914-1918 war'

In 1925, Wesley, at eleven years, was enjoying the sprawl of Strumpshaw's Old Hall Farm. Albert, his father, had taken on the tenancy for the Holmes family after the passing of the last squire, William Charles Flower Holmes. It was here that Wesley bought his first steam engine at the age of sixteen and as he said in 1981 "I've mucked about with them ever since". By 1930 his 'mucking about' led to an apprenticeship with Wiggs of Barnby, notable agricultural engineers and the skills acquired brought him back home when he took Manor Garage at Brundall in 1936.

Two months into the Second World War, Wesley Spanton Key married Ellen Mary Flower Holmes. The new Mrs Mary Key was the only child of the late William Holmes, and being a daughter she had signed the estate into a trust on the advice of her guardian at the age of twenty one. She felt the

Wesley Key in command of the Boxing Day shoot, 1983.

Nigel and Wesley Key c1920.

Kurt Angelrath marries Kiki Key, the granddaughter of William Holmes, April 1966.

The marriage of Edna Key to Philip Milner. Wesley Key, the bride's brother, stands to the right and her father Albert Key, with spectacles, stands fourth from right.

marriage to the son of her mother's estate manager would provide a sense of security.

The Keys set up home at Caister St Edmund and later Honing and Wesley became a farmer. But he kept his heart for steam forever pumping; preserving a few inherited engines which formed the nucleus of a collection. Wesley Key claimed he had no great passion for steam engines; simply that they had always been part of his life and would remain so. In 1954 he moved the collection to Strumpshaw and so began Strumpshaw Steam Museum.

As a committed preservationist he involved himself with the formation of the Norfolk Steam Engine Club with its first rally at Woodton Hall, Bungay in 1959. The event grew from a handful of enthusiasts, like Wesley, to become a regular meeting until the death in 1969 of the rally's founder, G C Howlett. From that time Wesley played host to the rally in the park at Strumpshaw and so began the village's association with the steam preservation movement.

By this time the Keys had returned to live in Strumpshaw. Mrs Holmes, Wesley's widowed mother-in-law, had died in 1960 and Mary was happy to be back in Strumpshaw. There were people and roots here that she had been unhappy to leave and now there was a family: son James and daughter Kiki. The lineage of Strumpshaw steam seemed secure for another generation.

A pioneering exhibitor at Strumpshaw's first rally was David King. Through an appearance on Anglia Television's "Bygones" programme he became a local celebrity, building steam boilers for all manner of applications, earning him the title King of Steam. For his attendance at a subsequent rally with a McLaren 6hp traction engine a television crew followed him the 20 miles to Strumpshaw from his Suffield home:

'One particular occasion, on the way, I was coming up one of the hills just this side of Wroxham and the 'big ends' started to tighten up. I didn't want to stop on the hill so I opened the throttle and she really barked and pulled up the hill. I just got to the top when the cameraman came running up and said, 'that was wonderful, can you do that again?' It took me about five hours!'

Tucked away in the back of the Old Hall's farmyard, Strumpshaw Steam Museum began to grow. Wesley welcomed visitors from May to September beginning with the Bank Holiday rally when around 10,000 people came through the gates during the three day event. The museum suspended the motion of a stately age when England produced the finest engi-

"King of Steam". David King at the 2009 rally.

neering in the world. The collection grew to become a rescue centre for engines and farm equipment, destined for the scrapyards. The mass of acquisitions highlighted Strumpshaw Steam Museum as the largest private collection in the country.

History is stored there: Buller a heavy traction engine saw service in the Boer War, its name taken from Sir Redvers Henry Buller (1839-1908) who had commanded 70,000 men during the South African war in 1899. The engine was used to haul six ton trailer-loads of ammunition and was returned to England after 1902. In another corner stands a set of

A volunteer keeping the engines going at Strumpshaw Museum in 1981.

Three generations at Strumpshaw Steam Museum, September 1982: Left to right: Wesley Key, son Jimmy and grandson William. (PICTURE BY COURTESY OF EASTERN DAILY PRESS)

Wesley Key on the footplate of Ginette Marie, June 1982.

Steaming by the church for Wesley Keys's Thanksgiving Service, 12 October 1995.

The Addington beam engine, standing as high as a house in Strumpshaw Steam Museum.

threshing tackle which had seen service on the estate as recent as 1962. But pride of the place was given to Princess Royal a rebuilt showman's engine.

A passionate acquisition in 1979 was Ginette Marie, a narrow gauge railway locomotive. She was German-built in 1937 for quarry work and brought to England in 1970 for carting materials for a new power-station under construction in Wales. A mile of track bought from the former Norfolk and Suffolk River Board was laid through Strumpshaw Park without felling a single tree. The result was a few tight bends but as Wesley said at the time: "We'll have to knock them out". The track alone was historical having seen service during bank rebuilding work following the terrible North Sea Surge of 1953. For a few years from 1982 Ginette Marie steamed around the mile long circular track to the delight of visitors before taking up permanent residence in the museum.

In 1981 a chance remark by three visitors to the museum put Wesley into full steam mode. Two massive beam engines at Thames Water's Addington Pumping Station, built in 1893, became redundant in

Wesley Key's Thanksgiving Service, 12 October 1995. Left to right: Kiki Angelrath, Rebecca Key, William Key, Jimmy Key.

1975. Both engines were the subject of a public enquiry because Thames Water wanted to demolish the listed buildings which housed them. The Secretary of State for the Environment intervened and several museums expressed interest in taking one of them, with Strumpshaw on the list. Negotiations brought months of frustration for Wesley Key and inspections of his museum by the London's water authority and council. Long term security of the engine was their concern but after much soul searching, Strumpshaw was pronounced suitable for one engine.

The beam engine was dismantled and brought to Strumpshaw. Its historical significance and educational value laid in its example of Victorian designing. It became a point of pilgrimage for enthusiasts, just to see the 18ft diameter flywheel turning once more for sixteen times each minute and in the same time its pump had the power to deliver almost fifteen thousand pounds of water. In the absence of a steam source it was operated by compressed air for the benefit of visitors.

In 1993 the organising of the annual Strumpshaw steam event was taken over by the museum. More of the input was coming from Wesley's son Jimmy and in turn there was a fledgling interest from his son William. Some years were good and others not, as everything depended on the weather. Heavy engines on pasture after rain made the going very bad. Then

Katie Glass, Anglia Television Announcer, receives a £1000 cheque from Rebecca Key on behalf of Guide Dogs for the Blind, 31 October 1986. Left, is Kenny Gooch and his guide dog Delsa, while far right is Wesley Key, Rebecca's grandfather. (PICTURE BY COURTESY OF EASTERN DAILY PRESS)

Christine Weber of Anglia TV with Mary Key April 1988.

Chris Spinks, left, and William Key, 2009.

Stone crushing by steam at Strumpshaw Rally, 2009.

A majestic line-up at Strumpshaw, 2009.

Strumpshaw Rally's organising team in 2009. Left to right, back row: Paul Worbey, William Key, Sarah High, Jack Angel, Pip Parker, Mark Worbey, Julia Jones' mother, Tony Rumball, Brian James. On engine: Chris Spinks, Rupert Liss. Front: Julia Jones, Lynn Worbey, Sarah Worbey, Vanessa Sayer.

Strumpshaw Steam Rally, 2009.

in 1995, on 3 October, Wesley Key passed this life.

The museum is Wesley Key's memorial but his commitments to the farming community have gone unsung. He was a member of the Smallburgh Internal Drainage Board and became verbal in promoting the need for the Yare Barrier to safeguard the farming environment: "We don't want the ruddy sea up as far as Norwich" he once said. Mary, his wife, predeceased him in 1989 but during their years together they raised £50,000 for their favourite charity, Guide Dogs for the Blind.

The untimely death of son Jimmy at the age of 58 on 24 April 2006 threw his son William a challenge. The burden was equal to that experienced by his great-grandfather William Charles Flower Holmes, when he inherited the Strumpshaw estate in 1908.

In 2009 William Key mixed with the throngs of visitors to the rally. Supporting, was Paul Worbey, the rally's organiser and like so many before, he had been bitten by the steam bug for which there was no antidote. Paul was an exhibitor and no stranger to Strumpshaw: one of those events he would never leave.

The 2009 rally was blessed with perfect weather. An early arrival, two days before the event, was Andy Potter and Derek Kirk who spent almost six hours covering the sixteen miles from Tunstead to Strumpshaw with their Foster engine. Princess Royal, Jimmy Key's showman's engine was in steam

once more, in the dedicated hands of Chris Spinks from Wymondham, one of the rally's many volunteers. Ernest Eagle from Ipswich considered the camaraderie of Strumpshaw steam was wonderful. He was a visitor and exhibitor of thirty years and considered the rally an annual reunion:

'I remember Jimmy from a little lad. He didn't mess about. What you saw is what you got. If you had to claim for an accident, for example, you might have

Keith Honour (left) receives the trophy for Best Exhibit from William Key at Strumpshaw Steam Rally, May 2009.

An engine from Tunstead arrives in Strumpshaw for the 2009 rally.

parked under a tree and a bough fell on the roof of your caravan and he'd say, "You were ruddy stupid to park under a tree, it's your fault". Then he'd go home and put a cheque in the post!'

The Strumpshaw Steam Museum is also home to a former cinema organ. The Christie, occupying a 'cuckoo in the nest' inhabitance with steam and agriculture, began life in a Reigate. It was installed at Strumpshaw after brief stays in Kings Lynn and Wellingborough. In June 2001 the organ was played by 92 year old Jackson Buick, the instrument's former organist who sat at the keyboard for the first time in 32 years. Then along came Lizzie Soanes, a teenager studying music at

Norwich City College, who was equally adept at making the museum reverberate to the sounds from the Christie. Paul Greenwood, famously known as organist at the Opera House, Blackpool, was happy to travel across country to Strumpshaw and give several performances. It all happened when he was holidaying in Norfolk and called in for a sneak play. Jimmy Key heard him and said, "What are you doing next Bank Holiday weekend and Christmas?"

The pinnacle of recognition for Jimmy came in May 2003. Fred Dibnah, that stalwart admirer of England's greatest engineering achievements, chose Strumpshaw Steam Museum for part of his television series.

Giles Peart, with his mother Julie, gets to grips with a half-scale traction engine, "Old Nick", under the eye of Ernest Eagle at Strumpshaw Steam Rally, 2009.

Paul Greenwood from Blackpool.

Jimmy Key (left) meets Fred Dibnah during his visit to Strumpshaw for recordings of a television programme in May 2003.

117

Chapter 17

◇

The Wood from the Trees

Strumpshaw is written as Stromessaga in the Domesday Book of 1086. Shaw is known to be an old English word for wood while Strum, some authorities say, might have derived from Anglo Saxon for stream, or even someone's name. It was also spelt as Strumpsal on a chalice. In every case, nobody really knows what Strumpshaw means but we can be sure that the village is home to some fine woodland.

In 1854 John Tuck Barnes proudly owned a medal presented to his grandfather in the previous century, honouring his improvements to the estate by planting fir trees. The work he carried out was in evidence a hundred years later although there are few fir trees now.

When Strumpshaw Hall's park was surveyed in 1880 there were five plantations of mixed specimens totalling about 30 acres. They had names; Top, South, Fosse, Leg of Mutton and Hazel. The last was planted specifically to produce 'brotches', the pegs used to hold bunches of reeds in place on thatched roofs. The reed was harvested from the fen and many houses in the village and the church once had roofs of thatch.

The plantations in the park were strategically placed to create a game shooting environment. When William Holmes bought the estate in 1881 he hated having cattle graze in the park fearing the damage they might inflict on the trees.

Ernest Hoyos in Mill Road's "avenue".

Strumpshaw's roadways are blessed with some fine looking trees, little more than thirty years of age. A good example is Mill Road where at the height of the growing season a tunnel of foliage provides shade and a most pleasant walk. Until the early 1970's the road along with many others in the village was almost devoid of trees as felling and hedge removal enabled farmers to crop as much land as possible

The roadside trees are now a part of the village's heritage. While we may take them for granted they resulted from the enthusiasm of one man, Ernest Hoyos, who moved to neighbouring Buckenham in 1971. Ernest and wife Coral fell for Sunny Cottage because its garden supported an established asparagus bed and there were three foot high oak saplings growing nearby. Those little trees were the nucleus of the avenues we see around Strumpshaw today.

Ernest's pioneering spirit needed support from the landowners. He started by talking to farmer, Geoffrey Youngs, who agreed to some being "popped in" along the verges of his fields. He thought Ernest was unlikely to see them in his lifetime. Other farmers agreed to the same proposition then welcome support came from the Tree Council of England with its "Plant a Tree in '73" campaign. Times were changing, with farmers, the government and the population beginning to appreciate the value of trees.

The garden at Sunny Cottage became a sapling nursery. Oak was the main crop as they were the trees of the area and the best for conservation, supporting most of the wildlife. There was ash and hornbeam although experts insist that Norfolk was on the northern limits for the latter. Elms were planted but the disease remains rampant.

Planting locations were important. Ernest found the area blessed with wide verges which allowed the trees to be set two metres back and never near the inside of bends, a point to be appreciated by motorists. A small amount of vandalism and the occasional nibbling by wild deer stunted some growths although oaks were good at sprouting new tops.

Tree planting of this nature was dependant on total devotion. The drought years of 1975-76 found Ernest visiting the sites of his plantings with car and trailer carrying cans of water to quench the thirsty saplings. It was a question of water them or lose them and his attention was rewarded: Stone Road, Long Lane and Buckenham Road now have trees twenty or thirty feet high. Ernest may not see them mature in his life time but the future generations will see the results of his work.

One group of those future generations were the last pupils at Strumpshaw School. When it closed in December 1980 the children and teachers were present for the planting of a horse-chestnut, on the green area opposite the school. The sapling had been grown from a conker which fell from its parent tree in Aylsham Road in Norwich close to where Ernest had once worked.

While the nurturing of trees was happening in Strumpshaw the whole nation was adopting similar projects. The supporters who promoted planting in 1973 wanted the scheme to continue so in 1974 the Tree Council was born. A way forward was to establish a "tree warden" in every locality now that trees were considered part of England's heritage. Tree Wardens are volunteers, generally appointed by parish councils, and currently number eight thousand in the country. The village's first warden was David Fagg.

Strumpshaw's current Tree Warden is Alasdair Fraser. His brief extends from being called for advice to keeping a watchful eye on trees around the village and reporting to officers at district level. He takes the front line for problems ranging from disease to

Ernest Hoyos with the horse-chestnut tree in Long Lane, planted in 1980.

unsympathetic pruning and felling. The role is not strictly a policing operation but rather fitting in as time sees fit, considering the job is voluntary.

As the RSPB's arboriculturist at Strumpshaw Fen Alasdair does notice things. It might be people pruning trees badly so he is happy to advise on the correct ways. He is far travelled from his childhood Edinburgh and fifteen years working in Reading to caring for the wet grazing marshes at Strumpshaw and meadows at Buckenham and Cantley.

Tree planting has been synonymous with Strumpshaw ever since the grandfather of John Barnes was rewarded with a medal. The most recent champion has been Mike Page who started planting in 1993. Behind his motor repair business in Norwich Road he created a three acre woodland to rival Eden, driven by a lifelong interest in wildlife. Testimony to Mike's conservation work was inclusion in the National Garden Scheme calendar of places worth visiting.

Alisdair Fraser, Strumpshaw's tree warden, 2009.

Chapter 18

Roads, Footpaths and
a Long Lane Awinding

Strumpshaw's roads were its earliest means of communication. They once were dusty tracks, used mostly by people on foot and horse drawn vehicles. There were numerous well-trodden paths crossing the village but when the lands were enclosed in the early 1800's some tracks acquired a right-angled turn, where a field was skirted. Many of the public footpaths displayed on the Ordnance Survey maps and enjoyed by ramblers, were once important routes while some are of dubious origin.

The village's main through route is Norwich Road. At the time of the enclosure in 1822 this thoroughfare was marked as Norwich Road until it reached The Goat (The Huntsman) then became Goat Lane as far as Lingwood. Confusion could be caused from the same map which also labels as Norwich Road the section of road passing the recycling site on what is now Stone Road. By the ordnance survey of 1882 that road had been designated Stone Lane and the section of Norwich Road from the bridge over the Lackford Run had become Long Lane where it wound its way to the top of the hill. From here, it continued as Norwich Road, the way it is today.

Cuckoo Lane, the meandering little road, uphill from the bottom of Long Lane was once called Braydeston Road. At the crossroads on Stone Road with Barn Hill the route to Strumpshaw Hall was called Staithe Lane; today it is Low Road. Map makers and surveyors of centuries past can be forgiven for the inconsistencies: none of the roads were signed and stayed as such for another hundred years.

More than two hundred years ago, Norwich Road crossed an important route, Ferrystye Way, at The Goat (The Huntsman). These days it survives as a pleasant rambling footpath, crossing the railway line, before continuing its way as Pack Lane. Its importance as a trade route was evident when the railway was laid through in 1883. The LNER installed a crossing and built a keeper's cottage to supervise passages as the lane was wide enough to take horse drawn vehicles. Pack Lane's junction with Chapel Road was then called Kittlewell Lane.

From 1841 when census records began to be taken every ten years, road naming did not improve. Norwich Road, through the top of the village, was called Goat Road, and sometimes Strumpshaw Road by the census enumerators up to 1891. Today's junction with Hemblington Road was known as Blofield Road or Lane, and occasionally, Blacksmith's Corner.

The Loke off the south side of Norwich Road had been known as Gymer's Loke and Fisher's Loke, due to its access to property owned by those families. Mill Road was never mistaken through its ascent to the windmill, while Chapel Road, at the crossroads with Lingwood, took its name from the opening of the Methodist Chapel in 1867.

Village signing and road names remained medieval until 1978. In that year the first six highways were permanently christened: Buckenham Lane, Buckenham Road, Hemblington Road, Long lane, Low Road and Norwich Road. The roads had

24 December 1984, Neville Burton fixes a new village sign, to replace the original given to the villages in 1968 by the Strumpshaw & Lingwood Women's Institute. Looking on, left to right: Sherry Bardwell, Ursula Harvey and Caroline Edwards.

The newly installed Coronation seat in June 1953. Note, Low Town Farm house in the background and a lack of trees.

Strumpshaw Guides in Buckenham Woods c1953. Left to right, back row: A Franks, A Stevens, Capt?, A short, C Wright. Front: J Cunningham, S Andrews?, Sally Curtis, B Beck, D Rose.

Madeline Broom (née Rose) left and sister Daphne Knights on the Coronation seat in 2009. They were present at the unveiling in June 1953.

121

never been labelled; just relying on the oral tradition of knowledge passed on through generations. Signs at the village entries came later and even then there was objection with one parish clerk seeing no need to be told where he lived!

The two signs which had informed travellers when they were entering Strumpshaw were gifts. The first, near the school, along with a commemorative seat, was installed to celebrate the coronation of Queen Elizabeth II in 1953, initiated by the Strumpshaw Girl Guides and supported by voluntary subscriptions. The second notice was at the crossroads with Lingwood. The double-sided sign was given by the Strumpshaw & Lingwood WI in June 1968 to commemorate the Golden Jubilee of their Norfolk Federation. Sadly, both signs have disappeared.

After the formation of Strumpshaw Parish Council in 1894 road mending appeared often on the agenda of meetings. At this time, the Surveyor of Highways for Blofield Rural District Council, James Curtis Waters, lived in the village at Brandon House so was on hand for advice or complaints.

A situation occurred in April 1914 regarding the Parish Gravel Pit. The quarry had been set aside under the Enclosures Act of 1904 to provide material solely for repairing of roads in the village but the Highways authority had been removing stones to mend roads in the district. The highways committee

was told that if stone was continually taken in this manner it would have to take full responsibility for all roads, including private roadways, in Strumpshaw.

The contractor for getting stone to the roads was Cornelius Waters. Before surfacing with granite chippings, so familiar on today's highways, the stone from Strumpshaw's gravel pit was used to keep the roads in repair and carted around in horse-drawn tumbrils. Cornelius owned six carts, often driven by men who went only by nicknames like "Wryneck Bob". The men were in the habit of calling at The Goat or The Shoulder of Mutton and as a result the stone was delivered short of its target!

The road to Strumpshaw's stone pits was aptly named. In 1926 Stone Road was widened to take the increased traffic to and from the gravel pit at the top of the hill, at a time when there really was no money for such work. The scheme was implemented to provide employment for men without work, for three days a week at eighteen shillings (90p). Wesley Key witnessed the fruitless operation:

'It was done just to find them something to do. I can remember them taking stone out of Buckenham stone pits and tipping it out of an old Foden lorry like the one in the museum. The two men would sit there all day breaking up the stone with hammers then afterwards carted it back to Buckenham. They just took it

The council steamroller by the junction of Hemblington and Norwich Roads c1925. The man on the far right, with bucket, is Ben Turner.

out for an occupation. That was in 1926 when things were really bad which led up to the General Strike. In those days tarmac wasn't in as we know it now. They used to have this old thin tar, in boilers, and pile the stones in heaps on the side of the road and lay the surface with a gang of about fifty men. We used to supply the horses to pull the tar "pods". One thing I never liked was the men wiping their tarred hands on the horses tails. The poor old beggars eventually lost their tails'

From those times the roads were kept in constant repair by the local roadman. 'Crump' Waters, the son of Cornelius, Strumpshaw's length-man, plied his skills from where he lived by the school, up as far as The Goat (Huntsman). He pushed a barrow laden with tools and materials to mend the holes, collecting his needs from the depot in Lingwood. This council yard also housed the local steam roller often seen in use during heavier repair work. Crump's patch took in Long Lane's winding course with its very high banks. They were removed in the 1960's with the spoil going to make up settlement on the Acle New Road. The lane's banks were then set back creating the present wide verges, in preparation to widen the road as a route to Cantley Sugar Factory. The scheme was abandoned and the lorries were sent elsewhere.

Long Lane has developed into a veritable conservation area. In 1987 the Blofield and District Conservation Group planted one hundred trees and shrubs on the south side, restoring a natural state which was lost during the widening process forty years ago.

Following years of campaigning Norwich Road was given a pavement followed by a 30mph speed limit. In 2009 one section remains unpaved between Beech Drive and the post office, having been added to the waiting list of Highways' projects.

The remnants of Strumpshaw's earliest communications can be found in its footpaths. From the 19th century these routes began to appear on Ordnance Survey maps and eventually totalled nineteen paths. A classic route is the track across the field from the Post Office Cottages at the top of Long Lane. This was directly trod between the churches of Strumpshaw and Braydeston from the time when the two parishes were annexed and the rector served both churches. From Cuckoo Lane the path picked up from High Noon Farm and became a Bier Way, the route once taken for a funeral cortege to Braydeston

Long Lane's verge is a nature reserve.

church and so the track was set.

The path from Barn Hill, across the field to Stone Road, was established as the stomping route of an 'old boy' from Low Town. Year in, year out he took this direct course to drink at The Shoulder of Mutton until the mapmakers from the Ordnance Survey adopted it as permanent. Like many footpaths, it was simply a case of treading a right of way. Once mapped, the route was there for all time.

In 1957, a Survey of Public Rights of Way was required under the National Parks and Access to the Countryside Act of 1949. At this time Strumpshaw supported 19 footpaths and the parish councils job was to see that they were kept in order and sign-posted. Footpaths were still held in historical high esteem but not often used as could have been. Well publicised annual walks were organised to keep the rights of way well trod and often there were complaints.

In 1961 the thoroughfare from The Huntsman to the railway crossing and beyond into Pack Lane was reduced in status to a 'public footpath' by the British Transport Commission. It was once an important route, but the crossing keeper's service had been withdrawn and the continued path beyond the railway was in a poor state. The parish council agreed to the change, giving today what is a pleasant country footpath.

During the Millennium celebrations of 2000, Norwich Road spawned a spectacle to herald each Spring. As the winter recedes snowdrops appear on the verges, seemingly growing naturally along the road as far as the post office. But the growth is far from natural; the flowers were carefully planted. The delightful harbinger of the year's first season was the idea of resident, Rita Bedford who responded to an appeal for schemes to mark the millennium. In 1999 Revd Vivien Elphick suggested the church and parish council unite, in respect of limited resources, to celebrate the milestone date. Rita Bedford's idea answered the criteria and the scheme was accepted.

Timing of the operation was important. The snowdrops had to be harvested and replanted after the flowers of 1999 had finished blooming. The plants were from Rita's own stock and with one or two volunteers all were in place along the verges for flowering in the year 2000. The snowdrops are low enough to withstand the rigours of the annual verge cutting although Rita keeps a watchful eye and each Spring fills any gaps. The display is a legacy to future generations and it came at no cost to the village.

Chapter 19

The Post Office

For more than 150 years one daily routine in Strumpshaw, the delivery of mail, has seen only basic changes. The village post office moved house a few times, the means of transport changed, but the postman always came knocking.

In 1854 the postmaster was John Spooner who combined the service with being the licensed 'victualler' of the Shoulder of Mutton. Here was situated Strumpshaw's post office where letters arrived from the sorting office at 10am each day and outgoing mail was despatched at 4pm. Letters came through neighbouring Burlingham where Charles Farman, the wheelwright and blacksmith received them at 8am to be sent on foot to Strumpshaw. In these early times the role of post master was always a secondary occupation.

By the 1880's the village post office had moved to a cottage next door to The Goat. William Harrison junr was the post master which he combined with being pork butcher and shopkeeper. As receiver of Strumpshaw's mail, on foot from North Burlingham, the service was now improved by letters arriving at 7-15am with mail out by 4-10pm. The building serving as post office was on the Lingwood side of the pub and has long been demolished.

William Harrison sold everything in his shop, from reels of cotton to joints of pork. As well as dealing with the mail, he went on rounds of the village delivering groceries with his trap, drawn by a pony called Duke. The family lived in the cottage now called Kenmare, next door to The Goat (Huntsman). William frequented Acle market to buy pigs for slaughter. The killing took place at the property's rear where a brick building with a beam running through with hooks to hold the animals while the blood ran away to a 'blood pit'. William, remembered as a large and happy man died at the untimely age of 49 so the business had to be sold.

Strumpshaw's next post office was at the top of Long Lane by the junction with Buckenham Road. Known at the time as 'the new post office', it was established in the east end of two cottages built in

William Harrison with his pony Duke, in Norwich Road.

1869 by Edward Barnes to house workers on his estate. One of the two ground floor rooms served as the post office, with a counter, chest of drawers but no safe. Sarah Dingle was the post mistress while her husband worked for the Barnes' at the Hollies as groom and gardener. Amongst a few wares, she sold paraffin oil, dispensed from five gallon drums, kept in a shed outside.

At the outbreak of World War I the village postman became a soldier and went to France. For the duration of the war, the Strumpshaw round was tread by a young woman, Alice Manthorpe. She lived in Pack lane where her grandfather was the coal merchant. Alice walked every road and footpath; morning, afternoon and evening, seven days a week, without a break for the entire war. She started at six in the morning and where possible used her cycle, against regulations, because Strumpshaw was a 'foot-round':

'The mail was brought to Burlingham by horse. Our bag came from Norwich and was picked up and sorted at Lingwood for Buckenham and Strumpshaw. I did it from the day war broke out because I'd been doing the Sunday duty for about a year before the war. I was on the spot so I was lucky to get the job. I went to Mrs

Post Office Cottages c1911.

The Post Office Cottages in 2007.

Alice Manthorpe in new uniform c1914.

*Dingle's in the morning to pick up there. There was
one box at Strumpshaw Post Office and another at the
Hollies: a letter box at the gate, take theirs out and put
mine in. Mind you, that was the war time so there
were seven pound parcels. If I had to go to Braydeston
I'd got to carry them on my back, right across to the
farm at High Noon and that was my lot in the
morning. In the afternoon I had to clear the box at the
Workhouse and in the evening I had South
Burlingham to do with a box there. Once when we
had snow there wasn't a soul who had been from
Strumpshaw Hall up to the mill, on the old Stone
Road. I'd got snow in my boots so my feet were wet so
I had to shuffle along. As soon as I got home I'd got to
dry out and go on the Lingwood round'*

In bad weather, Alice rarely received a thank you at
the furthest points of delivery, yet close to home
someone might give her sixpence (2.5p).   At
Christmas, with the added weight of parcels, she was
helped by Dr Smith with his pony and trap. He lived
in Lingwood at the Sand Hole and was hired by the
post office.

Letters came direct from Norwich to
Strumpshaw's new post office and it could receive
telegrams.   In the days of few telephones the
telegram was the best means for vital communication, particularly for relaying urgent or bad news.
On receiving a telegraphed message on her machine,
Mrs Dingle would keep an eye for boys coming up
Long Lane on their way home from school. She
would apprehend a willing lad to deliver the
telegram, generally for the agreed fee of threepence,
a fraction more than 1p in the present currency. The
telegram, issued from its receiver as a paper strip
with the message printed along its length, was cut
into short sentences and pasted onto a form. Dudley
Rowland once walked to Blofield with one such
message for three-pence, having negotiated, unsuc-
cessfully for a shilling (5p).

Sarah Dingle was remembered as a tall, kindly
lady but often unwell in her later years. Kathy Mills
from Oaklands Farm remembered her during the
Second World War:

*'I went in there once and she was complaining
because service men's wives got their allowances at
the post office during the war. All the men had been
called up in the forces so she had to pay out, "You
know, I have a lot more to do now, paying out the
money for the soldier's wives' and children but I still
get only six pounds a month. They don't give me any
more for doing all the money" she said.'*

Mrs Dingle died in February 1948 at the age of 79
years and with her passing the post office closed. Its
next home was in one of the cottages behind the
present post office where it was run in a small room
by Mr Lee. Then Mr Gant arrived and he eventually
built the last office, mostly as we know it today, on
the land which had been the pasture for William
Harrison's pony.   With the development of the
welfare state the village post office became an important centre. But the service remained secondary to
another business which without, there would be no
post office; just as had been a century ago.

The Post Office was associated with the early telephone system but there were few subscribers in
Strumpshaw. The telephones were operated through
a manual exchange at Enfield Cottage in The Street at
Brundall; hence all the numbers were headed
Brundall. There were just seven lines to Norwich and
two positions on the local switchboard covering
Blofield, Brundall, Lingwood and Strumpshaw with
a total of 200 subscribers. Calls to other exchanges
and long distance "trunk calls" were routed through
Norwich.

Amongst the subscribers were Albert Key at Old
Hall Farm with No 19; Arthur Colman, Blacksmith
No 40; Shoulder of Mutton No 44 and Alfred
Brighton at The Goat No 176.   The number for
Cantley factory had been routed into Brundall as it
could not connect with the system at Freethorpe.

Strumpshaw born Doris Batchelor worked at the
exchange in 1937 from the age of 16. She had taken a
General Post Office exam and oath of secrecy as a
condition of becoming an operator.   The process was
simple; the caller lifted the handset of the telephone
and gave their requested number to Doris who then
dialled and contact was made.

At the outbreak of the second war Doris's father
and mother, Bertie and Lily Batchelor took over the
exchange.   The family had lived in Hollies Farm
cottage on Buckenham Road where Doris and two
brothers were born. Bertie Batchelor was the local
representative for Pearl Insurance and is credited for
owning the second motor car in Strumpshaw.

During the second war the exchange had to be
manned 24 hours with the family taking turns on
night duty. Restrictions at the time meant callers
were given just five minutes on the telephone, and
ten for service personnel otherwise the plug was
pulled at the Norwich exchange. By now there was a
large military presence in Brundall so the army had
installed its own lines and their operator slept close
by on a camp bed during the night. Wesley Key was
an early user of the telephone service and recounted
one disadvantage:

Above: *Alice Manthorpe on her cycle round in Lingwood c1917.*

Alice Bunn née Manthorpe, Strumpshaw's post-woman during the 1st World War meets postman, Denis Wymer in 1981.

Doris Mayes in 2009. As 16 year old Doris Batchelor she was the voice heard by callers on the manual telephone exchange from 1939.

Tom Smith clears Strumpshaw's, historic, "George Rex" box in 1981.

Christine and Steve Hearnden, 2009.

Vincent Ball clears the Strumpshaw box in 2007.

'You might ring up somebody in Strumpshaw tonight and the old boy would but in and say, "That's no good you ringing him tonight because he's gone to so and so or perhaps you'll catch him in the Mutton". The local telephone exchange knew where everybody was. I can remember that because when the first bombs dropped on the hill in 1940 a press reporter rang Mrs Holmes at the Hall to get information but Mr Batchelor butted in and said that no information was to be given'

In 1959 the exchange operation was switched to the automatic system in Norwich. By this time the subscribers had reached 500 with some people served by a 'party line'. This meant two subscribers sharing a number and each call depended on who got to the phone first, as the bell would ring in both houses.

Like the pubs and the church, post office incumbents came and went. Tom Smith became Sub-postmaster in March 1978, arriving from Wicklewood where he started in the postal service. Tom and wife Phyllis are remembered with fondness and it was during their stay that the Federation of Sub-postmasters adopted the motto of 'Use it or lose it'.

Strumpshaw welcomed its most recent Postmaster, Steve Hearnden and wife Christine on 13 January 1999. A two-week training period ensued where the postal authority insisted on the undivided attention of the new postmaster but Steve Hearnden found it was impossible:

'The central heating boiler broke down, the plumbing and electricity needed attention and questions about all of them needed answers. The first Saturday we told the resident shop assistants, Carol and Sandra that we would manage the shop on our own from 2pm, giving them a welcome break. The afternoon was extremely busy with the Lottery terminal in full use but with the number 5 button not working properly. The newspaper bills needed sorting along with general sales of groceries and the like. It seemed that all the customers had planned to visit us that afternoon just to see what the new owners were like! We fumbled our way through the session, collapsing in a heap, in the kitchen at 8pm. The mistakes we made were many but Carol and Sandra sorted them during the following two days'

The Post Office Stores began to develop and a bright future seemed inevitable. The shop and office became fully computerised, a licence to sell alcohol helped with growing competition from elsewhere. In due course government changes were introduced

enabling allowances, like pensions, to be paid to recipients without a visit to the post office. This furthered eroded the village's sure meeting place already under threat from the competitive supermarkets so closure of the shop came at the end of 2007. Then more battling ensued as the Post Office operation and the Lottery terminal came under threats of closure. These were saved but a subsequent letting was unsuccessful. Now with stationery, gifts, flowers and wines the post office is looking to the future once more.

For more than 150 years the postal service has remained constant. The technology, transport and delivered items may have changed but the postman still comes every day. Mail posted to Strumpshaw makes its first stop in the early hours at Blofield Post Office where bags of letters are broken down for sorting. Half is sorted by the time the postmen arrive at 6am for the ten rounds in this area; five on cycles and five in vans. They used to start an hour earlier but the Royal Mail needed to cut back on the costs of delivering.

Vincent Ball started twenty one years ago when postmen still wore a uniform of blazer with matching trousers and compulsory tie. Shorts were never allowed. He took the job by accident after being without work for about three months and his father just happen to speak to the postmaster. Vincent's van round of four hundred and ten calls starts in Blofield at Braydeston Drive, before moving on to Lingwood and Strumpshaw. The first eleven years he was on a cycle and noticed the vast changes in his time:

'I very rarely see handwriting. Personal letters have almost disappeared. It's mostly advertising material. We get leaflet drops about three times a week. People used to write to each other but there are very few such letters now. I used to have pen and paper for 'signed for' items, then came bar-codes but now it's by a scan gun. There used to be a man on collections but I have to empty the boxes on Chapel Road, Norwich Road, Shoulder of Mutton and the Post Office. When the hours changed I was turning up later so some people moaned. They didn't want their post at 1-30 in the afternoon'

A few residents may wish they received their post before breakfast. There are those who hate unsolicited mail and have an allergy to rubber bands, which postmen may drop unintentionally. But perhaps people should consider the service which has been with us for more than a hundred years and think of a future where the postman may not come knocking.

Chapter 20

◇

All Work and a Little Play

Try to imagine a life with very little leisure time. For Strumpshaw's folk, as far back as living memory can recall the only break in a week of relentless labour was Sunday. Various social gatherings were organised for churchgoers but the centre for many pastimes was at either of the two pubs, The Goat and The Shoulder of Mutton.

Outdoor entertainment was organised occasionally. On 9 January 1895 a football team from Strumpshaw was assembled to meet an eleven from the Blofield & Brundall Athletic Club, trained by Stanley McKelvie. The village had no recreation ground so a field was lent by Edward Barnes who lived at the Hollies and owned much of the land. The event was reported in the Blofield Deanery Magazine:

'The Blofield and Brundall boys showed good form and in the first half of the game scored 3 goals to 1. Although the snow lay thick on the ground the play was kept up pluckily on both sides to the finish, though no further points were made. Strumpshaw had unfortunately to play short in consequence of the heavy roads, which made some of the players late in arriving'

Soon after World War 1 the Strumpshaw Sports Committee was formed. A meeting of village notables decided to establish an annual sports day for Strumpshaw and district to take place on the Monday of Whitsuntide. We know it today as the Spring Bank Holiday. A well publicised gathering in 1921 was held in a field lent by farmer, Frank Futter and despite many other attractions on the same day the event was well attended. It made the columns of the Eastern Daily Press:

'The programme consisted of seventeen events, including a hackney horse race, which was a new departure for these sports, and caused much excitement, the result being 1st Frank Futter, 2nd Fred Atkins, 3rd Ralph Lemon. During the afternoon the

inmates of the Lingwood Union were entertained by Mrs Holmes, Strumpshaw Hall and tea was provided for them on the ground. Guessing competitions, including the weight of two pigs, caused considerable amusement. After the sports, dancing was enjoyed on the Revd B S Spurgin's lawn at the Rectory'

The Strumpshaw netball team, 1935. Left to right, back row: Sybil Williamson, Doris Batchelor, Edna Cowles, Agnes Wilby, Emily Barrett. Front row: Kathleen Horner, Iris George, Elsie Church.

By 1935 the committee comprised of an illustrious list of Strumpshaw names: a group of men who had emerged as driving forces through business and genuine concern for the social well-being of the village. They met frequently in either the Parish Room or the club room of The Goat. Thomas Atkins took the chair and presided over Mr Bland, Mr Etheridge, Herbert Mayes, John Newruck, Cecil Rope, Charles Mills, Charles Beck, Harold Broom, Robert Howes, Alfred Brighton, Basil Rope, Henry Moy and Jack Edwards. With industry and endeavour they set about making the Whit Monday Sports a permanent fixture on the calendars of Strumpshaw.

Eventually the sports event was given a permanent home in the grounds of Strumpshaw Hall.

A fête at Strumpshaw Hall c1924.

Albert Key, the estate manager, had been coerced into participating by agreeing to the use of the park while Miss Barnes of the Hollies organised refreshments. After each Whitsun event the group began fund raising for the next season by holding a whist drive in the parish room.

The list of events shows just how a village entertained itself in that period between the wars: 100 yards Mens Race, 75 yards Ladies Race, Fancy Dress, Egg & Spoon, Sack Race, Shoe Mixing, Baby Show, Tug-of-war, Bicycle Race, Three Legged Race, 75 yard Married Ladies Race, 100 yards Men Over 40 and Cigarette Lighting! For those not running or jumping there was bowls, hoop la, guessing the weight of a pig, hidden treasure and Aunt Sally.

One of the most popular side shows to evolve was the Coconut Shy, a favourite of the fairgrounds. Harold Broom was charged with acquiring one hundred coconuts and Strumpshaw's blacksmith, Herbert Colman manufactured twenty irons on which the coconut targets were placed. Participants at the event would hurl a solid wooden ball to dislodge the nut from its perch and claim it as the prize. The side-show became so popular that the irons were loaned to other event organisers.

Strumpshaw's sporting prowess produced one athletic celebrity. Percy Feek, born 1914 showed

Percy Feek, 1938.

early promise as a runner and was coached by Frank Futter one of the sports committee pioneers. There are memories of Percy pounding the roads through the village and anyone ever intent on beating him needed a considerable head start.

In August 1931 Percy Feek joined the 2nd Battalion Norfolk Regiment where his skill as an athlete was noticed and promoted. At 19 he was a prized member of the Battalion's cross country team and helped it to the unbeaten championships of 1933-34. He won the Devon County Cross Championship for his regiment in 1934 and took first place in the 10 mile race at the Aldershot Command Athletic Association. When the Battalion was posted to Gibraltar he came first in the 1937 cross country. On return to England, Percy entered the Norfolk County AAA Championship and took a worthy 2nd in the two miles flat race, on 23 July 1938.

With the outbreak of the second war in 1939 the Whit Monday sports needed police approval to go ahead as was the rule regarding any public assembly. Two meetings were held at Oaklands within a week in 1940, when it was agreed that free admission be granted to men serving in the forces. Whit Monday's event of that year was the last to be held as World War 2 seemed to have clouded Strumpshaw's annual gathering.

During the Second War the village was entertained by its own variety troupe. Sixteen year old Frank Futter, son of Oaklands farmer, Frank Senr instigated a concert party in collaboration with Ron Mingay, calling themselves "The Lingwood Follies". The idea was born of the need to occupy themselves and bring

The Lingwood Follies c1940. Left to right, back row: Alfie Becket, Mary Curtis, Irene Edwards, Albert Edwards, Joan Lyons, Neville Goose, John Lake. Front: Betty Rose, Frank Futter, Alf Goose, Ronnie Mingay, Betty Futter.

some cheer in the dismal time of war.

Betty Rose, later to become Betty Warman, contributed accordion along with friend Betty Futter, Frank's sister. They engaged a comedian, Alf Goose who had moved to Lingwood from Norwich to escape the air raids, although he still travelled into the city everyday to work! The assembled group included Alf Beckett, as back-room boy; Mary Curtis, Irene Edwards, Joan Loynes, Neville Goose and John Lake. The troupe met and rehearsed in the recreation ground hut at Lingwood. Ron Mingay's mother made the costumes and found them a piano which was transported on a handcart between venues.

Strumpshaw's barn on Barn Hill and Futter's Barn (now a house in Beech Drive) was the venue on occasions. The Follies raised money for War Weapon's Week and played to audiences who sat on chairs borrowed from the parish and Reading Rooms. The show was taken round the locality to Beighton, Postwick, Brundall, Buckenham, Reedham and Cantley. Towards the end of the war the troupe wound up when Alf Goose returned to Norwich and Frank Futter joined the RAF.

Strumpshaw for a while even had a taste of theatre and cinema. An old barn, on Barn Hill, now demolished, became a centre for entertainment when it served as a canteen worked by volunteers during the second war. The building, part of Hollies Farm, was equipped with a stage and provided a welcome retreat for soldiers stationed nearby. Bunches of

straw often served as seats but that was part of the fun. Concerts were held there and during the 1950's a travelling film exhibitor would set up a show on Friday nights. Mary Jermy, then courting Ronald Forder, enjoyed going there to see Laurel and Hardy and Lew Warman saw a "Humphrey Bogart" on one occasion. The cinema shows were staged alternately with others in Blofeld and Terry Atkins remembers the place being got ready for his sister Dot's wedding reception. The barn was simply swept out and made ready for any event.

One of those events was a visit from "Professor Grenies Peepshow". The conjuror and ventriloquy act had been engaged for a children's party and included a young entertainer, singer and pianist, Rita Roe, from Norwich. She had been signed up from Madame Osina's Dance Troupe, which during the war put on shows at numerous military encampments around the county. It was the budding performer's first visit to Strumpshaw until she returned years later to reside permanently, as Rita Marriot, the wife of Arthur, the council's Water Inspector.

A night out in Strumpshaw was often completed by a visit to the fish and chip shop. The wooden hutted 'chippy' was being run in 1944 by Mr W H Forder and situated in an opening in the lane by the side of the current post office. It was later operated by the Stygall family who also set up the frying business in Lingwood. Terry Atkins recalled: "the old man was the best fryer I had ever known". The quality needed to be good as the service could be slow. Mary Nurse who lived close by in Kenmare was a customer:

'I remember always getting our fish and chips at Friday teatime. Mr Stygall would always give me a few chips in a bag while I waited in the queue'

Theatrical productions appeared at the barn in 1946 with The Strumpshaw Players. The local drama group was centred on the village's school teachers along with some of the local notables. Dorothy Watling of Church Cottage, relative of Norwich's Geoffrey Watling, produced the play while F C Symonds, having supplied the "theatre" was stage manager, assisted by Eric Redgment. Their production, "The Late Christopher Bean", was performed for three days, 11-13 April 1946, with its cast comprising of William Devenish the rector, Marjorie Ward, Barbara Buckton, Margaret Symonds, Joyce Ward, Cecil Platten, Harry Balders, Ernest Spooner and Eliot Blake, the local doctor.

The Sports Committee had been in hibernation

Rita Marriot, 2009, reflects on the time when stardom came very close and still entertains those confined to community centres.

Rita Roe, c1944.

Programme for The Strumpshaw
Players, 1946.

Strumpshaw Brownies c1954. Left to right, back row: Elizabeth Coleman, Diane Rose, Christine Colman, Ingrid Monkman, Patsy Crowhill, Carroll Piggin. Front: Linda Everson, Jenny Wooler, Margaret Orford, Linda Baker, Pamela Sage.

since the start of the war. Then a glimmer of awakening came in October 1952 when the parish council was deciding how to celebrate the Queen's Coronation in June 1953. The rector at the time, Revd Brandwood, promoted his idea of providing a playing field for the village; the very same dream of the original sports committee. The response was that the rector could donate a bit of his Glebe but this came to nothing. The villager's rallied to the coming festivities and staged dances in Futter's barn in Beech Drive to raise money for any celebrations. The old building was cleared of debris and whitewashed for the occasion by Lingwood painter and decorator, Cecil Priestly.

The Strumpshaw Sports Committee had served well in its time but all that remained was a bank balance. A temporary committee was convened on 23 July 1970 to discuss a proposal from the Parish Room's trustees for a loan from the funds to enable them to build a new kitchen and toilets. The loan was made and the work was implemented. Soon after, the one surviving original trustee, Henry Moy, was told that the temporary committee had been set up without legal basis. Henry appointed the Parish council to be the trustee of the Village Sports Fund on 1 April 1972. From that time on the funds accrued interest in hopes that one day the village might have its own playing field.

The spirit of Strumpshaw's sporting past was rekindled, briefly, in 1987. In that year the newly-formed Norfolk Rural Community Council was given the task of organising the County Finals of the Inter-Village Sports Competition and Strumpshaw responded to the call. The intention was to raise

enough enthusiasm to enter a "knock-out" event at Sprowston on 30 May.

With little time to find a team everything depended on initial contact with known sporting

Henry and Rosa Moy in 1979, celebrating their Diamond Wedding. Henry was the last member of the Strumpshaw Sports Committee. (PICTURE BY COURTESY OF EASTERN DAILY PRESS).

Inter Village Sports Competition, 4 July 1987. Strumpshaw's team, pictured here, was: Graham Howard, Jason Howard, Adrian Weavers, Nicky Dungar, Chris Harper, David Patterson, Tarina Bannon, Dorothy Hewitt, Barbara Blatch, Kate Blatch, Alison Peart, Lesley Smith, Jenny Fox, Carmel Blackburn, Diane Baker, Stephen Peart Junr, Lee Roberts, Dougal Cameron, Hamish Cameron, David Blatch, Adam Burroughs, Zoe Roberts, Claire Jenner, Claire Barker, Dawn Hewitt, Caroline Chilcott, Sarah Cullum, Nicola Page, Lee Johnson, Nina Burroughs, Angus Cameron, Joanne Bridgeman, Adrian Snowling, Frances Snowling, Norby Bothner, Eva Temple, Mark Burns, Sarah Burns, Duncan Cameron, Rita Bridgeman, Theresa Mulligan, Elizabeth Cameron, Susan Roe.

types. The request was for Five-a-side Football, Netball, Badminton and Table Tennis. Word soon spread and the response was surprising. Within days there were enough players to form the teams drawing on residents from the whole of Strumpshaw's parliamentary parish which encompassed Buckenham and Hassingham.

The footballers met first in the grounds of The Old Rectory on Sunday 10 May, coached by Strumpshaw's Bob Blyth, a former Lingwood player. From that first meeting Thursday was fixed as "football night" at Lingwood Playing Field. During the following week, the ladies netball teams, junior and senior, met at Brundall School, coached on the first occasion by Shelia Ashford. It was years since some of the girls had played but old skills soon returned. The badminton and table tennis teams were selected through willingness after a little persuasion and completed the Strumpshaw line-up.

By Saturday 30 May the Strumpshaw team was ready to take on the world but the only contenders were Rackheath and Woodbastwick. The seal of the

day was set by the senior footballers when they beat Woodbastwick 3-0. Netball, Badminton and Table Tennis won some and lost others and by the end of the afternoon totting up began to show that Strumpshaw had amassed several points. Strumpshaw and Rackheath tied but this village had sported complete teams, a statutory requirement of the competition. The reward of further points put Strumpshaw in the lead.

On 4 July the entire team travelled by coach to the Breckland Sports Centre at Thetford for the county final. Strumpshaw was pitched with the best teams in Norfolk from four other villages: Massingham, Neatishead, Tasburgh and Tilney. It proved an exhausting day, competing against teams with three or four year's experience to the few months of Strumpshaw. Without any shame the village team came bottom of the table but the fun had been in taking part in a competition in which the whole of Norfolk had been invited to participate. Of the five teams who had made it to the final, one had come from Strumpshaw.

Chapter 21

Foreign Fields; and Certain Death

Within a century of living memories no events had as much impact on Strumpshaw as the two world wars. A generation of young men was lost to some families in The First World War, or Great War as it is often known. It began with an incident in Sarajevo on 28 June 1914 when the Archduke Ferdinand of Austria was assassinated by a Serbian student. The event passed with little interest, especially amongst the people of this village. Who thought that a murder in Sarajevo would be the root of a world conflict which would affect Strumpshaw?

The Tunmore brothers; William (standing) and Frederick.

Why did England go to war? The world at that time consisted of rich, powerful and jealous nations. Germany, whose aggressiveness had been strengthening for forty years was an ally of Austria so it would have to punish Serbia for killing the Archduke. This was a good excuse to have a prod at Russia, Serbia's ally, in turn an ally of France.

In that era of land battles and marching armies, Germany's easy route into France would mean going through Belgium. But Germany, who by a treaty in 1831, had promised never to invade the harmless little nation, ignored the agreement and sent troops into Belgium. Britain, having promised to support the Belgian people in times of trouble, declared war on Germany, 4 August 1914.

England had little time to muster forces and aid Belgium. Voluntary recruitment had maintained an army but now an intensive campaign was implemented. "Your country needs you" was proclaimed in posters and newspapers which roused excitement everywhere.

Amongst the early recruits from Strumpshaw were the Tunmore brothers; Frederick 20 and William 17, who was under age. Recruiting sergeants were often not too questioning of age, if the recruit looked old enough, as they were paid bonuses for the numbers of men enlisted. The two boys joined the East Surrey Regiment and were happy knowing they would be together.

Their village life was idyllic as could be but with no preparation of what lay in store. Stephen Tunmore, their father, a 27 year old engine driver from Norwich had married Sarah Waters a 20 year old Lingwood girl in January 1890. The 1891 census records them as living in Workhouse Road, Lingwood with their four month old daughter, Laura. Son Frederick followed three years later then William was born in 1897. They moved house to live in Kittlewell Lane (now Pack lane), in a cottage next door to the Rope family who were fruit farmers in the village. From here the boys attended Strumpshaw School.

After enlistment Frederick and William were dispatched to Purfleet to begin training. This entailed every aspect of turning a young man into a soldier and above all the drilling and the grilling to instil total discipline. While at Purfleet Frederick wrote home to his father:

Rope family cottages, Pack Lane, c1940.

'We went for a long march this morning but I have not felt anything of my toe. (apparently he suffered an injury before enlisting) We have got blue uniform and white belts so they look alright'

While the Tunmores were becoming acclimatised to the rigours of training news came through of Strumpshaw's first war casualty. Private Robert Wilson, son of the late John and Hannah Wilson of Hemblington was killed in action on 29 October 1914. He was amongst the first soldiers sent to France with the 1st Battalion of the Norfolk Regiment and at the age of 41 years,

Alfred Rope in uniform of the Royal Garrison Artillery

was the eldest. With no known grave he is commemorated amongst the 53 members of the Norfolk Regiment on the vast memorial at Le Touret in France.

The war developed in a way not even its generals had foreseen. The murdering power of machine guns and the total destructive force of heavy artillery meant it was impossible for armies to stand and fight. They dug themselves into trenches which stretched across France from the Alps to the sea. The only way to engage the enemy was to climb out of the trenches and into the open to cross "no man's land" and become entangled in a forest of barbed wire which protected the opposing trenches. It was here the attackers would be mown down.

In the churchyard at Strumpshaw, Robert Wilson's name concludes the list on the village war memorial. Less than halfway down the roll of honour is Private William Harrison, Strumpshaw born, the eldest son of William Harrison the village's Sub-postmaster. William had enlisted in the Suffolk Regiment and left England for France on 26 January 1915. His was a short time to live and fight; being killed in action by 23 April

Against the knowledge of these early losses the two Tunmore boys continued training. They suffered extreme weather conditions, uncomfortable accommodation and shortage of equipment. At one point there were 100 rifles for a battalion's 1,100 men. So few great coats were issued that most men were wearing their civilian garments, right through the winter. Off duty periods proved a highlight of the training and one occasion was a trip into Grays, in Essex. Frederick sent home a postcard showing the High Street, to his sister Laura:

'You ought to see this street on Saturday night. It is lined with soldiers. Willie and I did 4 o'clock guard

and have nothing to do so we shall have such a fine time of it'.

An even better break for Fred was a few days leave and back to Strumpshaw. He could then call on Alice Manthorpe, an attractive young 24 year old woman. She was Strumpshaw's postwoman who had been delivering most of Fred's mail sent from France. More than eighty years later evidence emerged that they were betrothed to marry.

On return from one period of leave in May 1915 the 8th East Surrey's moved to Salisbury Plain for more intensive training. They also prepared for an inspection by King Gorge V at the end of June ahead of their secret battle front destination but by mid July France was the most likely.

The journey from Southampton to le Havre and Folkestone to Boulogne started on 25 July 1915. There was a further period of training in France where the unit became based, about fifteen miles from the Somme front. Excitement was now as such that Fred wrote home to his cousin George Tree in Chapel Road imploring him to enlist and join them in France and in due course he signed on with the Royal Field Artillery.

By 1915 thirty one of Strumpshaw's boys had volunteered for war service but August brought two more losses. John Debbage and Ernest Rose were drowned in the Aegean Sea when their troop ship, Royal Edward, was torpedoed and sunk on the 13 August. Ernest and John had listed in the Norfolk Regiment but were amongst three hundred men who volunteered to transfer to the Essex Regiment. With no grave they are commemorated on the Helles Memorial along with more than 850 men lost when the Royal Edward sank.

Meanwhile in France the East Surrey's had been placed in a relatively peaceful part of the line; a simple ploy to enable new arrivals to gain confidence. All were being prepared for the Somme offensive.

The Tunmore boy's experienced the hell of machine gun and rifle fire on 1 July 1916. They left the safety of the trenches to press toward objectives but after emerging with their lives there was rest before more action in the coming months. In April 1917 there was more training to prepare for the effects of tear-gas shells and fighting in the open. The division was soon to take part in the Battles of Arras and unbeknown to the Tunmores, other Strumpshaw

Anna Tree with children, Olive and Cecil, August 1917.

Left: *George Tree, December 1916, a driver with the Royal Field Artillery.*

Two Strumpshaw soldiers, photographed together, who never came back. Pte Ernest Rose (left) who died at sea in August 1915 and Pte John Edward Blake, a Lance Corporal by the time of his death in 1918.

The Atkins brothers. Left to right, standing: Richard, Fred. Sitting: Harry, Tom.

The grave, in Belgium, of William Tunmore.

138

men were stationed close by; brothers Fred, Harry and Richard Atkins of the 12th Lancers were preparing for the same battle.

After journeying on foot and by train the East Surrey's reached the front line half a mile from a place called Cherisy. The attack was launched along a front of sixteen miles. The daily casualty rate was higher than the famous Somme battle with 5,000 men dying on 3 May 1917; among them was Frederick Tunmore.

His surviving brother William with his 8th Battalion companions were moved back from the front line to relieve the pressure. By the 10 August 1917 the Surrey's went in support of the 7th Battalion 'Queens' came under heavy shell fire and lost thirty-eight men from amongst the ranks: William Tunmore was one of their number. He is buried at the Hooge Crater Cemetery, further along 'the road to death'; the Menin Road; the very road that had taken him to the front. In Strumpshaw Mrs Tunmore never recovered from the loss of her two boys.

The list of names on Strumpshaw's war memorial is headed by two more brothers, Alfred and Hugh Barton, sons of Rev Alfred Barton, rector for the years 1891-1917. Hugh Fabian Barton was born at Strumpshaw Rectory on 20 January 1897, the third and youngest son of Revd and Mrs A J Barton. From school he joined the Public School Corps and was appointed 2nd Lieutenant in the 9th Norfolks in September 1914. He was sent with his unit to France on 8 October 1915 and was soon engaging the enemy. Like all the volunteers for this war young Barton had been led to believe the battle would be won and everyone would be home for Christmas. But in December he sent an army issue Christmas card to Mrs Holmes at Strumpshaw Hall.

After four months of continuous fighting, with just a hospital break after suffering trench feet and some leave of six days, he was killed in action by shrapnel fire at the age of 19. His colonel wrote home to the Revd and Mrs Barton at Strumpshaw:

'It is with great sorrow that I have to write and tell you your dear son was killed in a moment by a shell on Saturday afternoon, about 5pm, on 12 February, in the first line of trenches. He was buried next morning a 7am at the small cemetery behind the lines by the side of our Norfolk men who lost their lives at duty's call. Our deepest sympathy goes out to you in the loss of that brave young life'

The rector's other son, Alfred Richard Barton, the elder, was already a veteran of military campaigns when the first war broke out. Born in Herefordshire before his father took up the Strumpshaw living he went to work in South Africa and joined the Southern Mounted Rifles to take part in the rebellion of 1904. Being in South Africa, in 1914, he pledged his support and returned to England with the 3rd Regiment South African Infantry, eventually being transferred to France where he was given his commission of Second Lieutenant. The regiment was engaged in the Somme Offensive at Delville Wood, the most famous battle for the brigade. Three thousand men from the battalion had entered the wood: only 768 came out unscathed. For a time there was hope that Alfred had survived but his body was found two days later. Another letter was received in Strumpshaw:

'I waited in the hope of getting news of your boy and only heard definitely yesterday from the 1st Gordon Highlanders that they had found the dear boy. He was an old friend of mine ever since the Boer War. We all loved his cheery jolly way. He was with me up to the 16th, well and hearty, when, owing to the terrible loss amongst the officers in the edge of Delville Wood, I had to send him up against an enormously superior force and under a terrific fire, but could not keep back the enemy, and he was last seen fighting hand to hand together with the few left in the trench'

Although these graphic accounts show that Alfred's body was found, like so many of his comrades he had no known grave and is commemorated on the Thiepval Memorial for the missing.

There were other theatres of war far away from the Western Front. Strumpshaw's Robert Hylton, of the village's blacksmith's family died on 31 March 1916 during the operation in Mesopotamia, 1914-21. With no known grave he is commemorated on the memorial at Basra. He was a private in the 2nd Battalion Norfolk Regiment.

William Thompson, son of George and Elizabeth Thompson, lived in The Loke. He joined the Norfolk Regiment and later transferred to the Essex Regiment. He has no known grave after dying in action, 14 April 1917 and is commemorated on the Arras Memorial in France.

Sergeant Robert Killington of the Army Service Corps came from a well established Strumpshaw family. He died 14 June 1917 and is buried in the Lahana Military Cemetery in the Balkans.

Two sons of Robert Howes, Strumpshaw's threshing contractor, went to war. Samuel was a fitter with the Royal Field Artillery and returned safely to maintain his father's business. But brother Arthur, who enlisted in the Norfolk Regiment, died 8 October 1917 having transferred to the Royal Warwickshire Regiment. His commemoration appears on the Tyne Cot Memorial in Belgium along with Lance Corporal John Blake of the Norfolk Regiment. He died 15 April 1918 aged 24 years, leaving a wife Marjorie living at nearby Postwick.

A most remarkable story recalled from the front involved Strumpshaw's blacksmith, Russel Peart. He lived in Chapel Road Lingwood but had taken the forge in 1909 after the passing of Robert Thrower. While at the battle front he had a chance meeting with Reggie Bunn from Burlingham, whose father had taught him the rudiments of the forge:

Pte Frank Ward of the Grenadier Guards, one of the few soldiers taken prisoner during the First World War.

'*Russel Peart was an exceptional good friend to me. I shall always remember him from the time we were both in France. I was in a situation that I'd nothing only what I stood in. I'd lost everything. I went through a village and came to a field hospital. Russel was in the Royal Army Medical Corps. There was a* field ambulance and I had to go past this and by an amazing chance I met Russel. It was a surprise meeting and he invited me to stop. 'Where's your kit' he said. 'I've lost the damn lot' I replied, 'everything and all I've got is what I'm standing up in'. 'We'll see what we can do'. So he gave me a pair of cavalry breeches and two jackets. On one the blood was all congealed, so hard and stiff. He helped me and here we were, all the way from Lingwood and Strumpshaw'

The last Strumpshaw soldier to die, on 23 August 1918, little more than two months before the Armistice, was Sydney Green. He was a Private in 1st Battalion Hertfordshire Regiment but had enlisted first into the Cambridgeshire Regiment. He was the son of John and Alice Green. Mary Key of Strumpshaw Hall recalled in 1981 how she was one of the last village people to see him alive:

'*His father was the gardener at the hall. Sydney came home on embarkation leave or something and*

Pte Vernon McLean of 8th Norfolks. He was Sgt McLean by the end of the war.

Russel Rope, Royal Field Artillery, 1915.

three days afterwards we heard he was killed. I was just a little girl but I can just remember it. It was at the end of the war. I remember his puttees; I was fascinated by his puttees'

By the time the armistice was signed in November 1918 sixty seven Strumpshaw men had gone to war: fifteen did not return. The village's first action was to record the names of all who had served and display a roll of honour in the church:

'Frederick Atkins, Harry Atkins, Richard Atkins, Thomas Atkins, Hugh Barton, Richard Barton, John Blake, Albert Broom, Harry Broom, Harold broom, Harry Brown, George Bullard, John Curtis, John Debbage, Percy Debbage, Fred Dingle, Charles Etheridge, Robert Farr, George Guymer, John Guymer, Sidney Green, Gordon Harper, Randall Harper, Arthur Harper, Alfred Harrison, William Harrison, Arthur Howes, Samuel Howes, Robert Hylton, Thomas Kealey, Alfred Kemp, Victor Kemp, George Killington, Robert Killington, Vernon McLean, Richard Mitchell, William Osborne, Arthur Palmer, Alfred Rope, Russel Rope, Ernest Rose, George Rose, Herbert Rose, John Rose, William Scott, Alfred Self, Albert Sutton, William Sutton, Ernest Thompson, George Thompson, Harry Thompson, Robert Thompson, William Thompson, Frederick Tunmore, William Tunmore, George Tree, Arthur Ward, Russel Ward, George Ward, John Ward, Frank Ward, Gordon Waters, Robert Wilson, Arthur Wilson, Arthur Wright, Albert Wright, J Wright'

The King decreed that every city, town and village should establish a permanent memorial to its fallen and Strumpshaw heeded the call. A vestry meeting on 4 July 1919 approved the design for a cross of Cornish granite bearing the dead soldiers names with its cost of £100 to be met by public subscription. Albert Rope organised the collection, assisted by Stephen Tunmore, the other churchwarden, who had lost his sons in the war.

The 8ft 6in high simple Celtic cross with crusader's sword in relief, carved in rough hewn Cornish granite was the work of G. Maile & Son, London's Ecclesiastical Craftsmen. The completed memorial was brought by rail to Lingwood Station, from where its two parts, the plinth and the cross, were transported by horse-drawn wagon to Strumpshaw churchyard.

On a Saturday 23 February 1920 the Bishop of Norwich came to Strumpshaw for the unveiling and dedication. A service in the church was conducted by the Rev Spurgin and addressed by the Bishop. The congregation included many relatives of the fallen and there were several uniformed soldiers and sailors present. The Rev Spurgin unveiled the cross and the Bishop dedicated it with a blessing and short prayer.

Wreaths were then laid in honour of the fifteen men: Alfred Richard Barton 34, Hugh Fabian Barton 19, John Edward Blake 24, John Debbage 21, Sydney John Green 20, William John Harrison 20, Arthur Robert Howes 19, Robert George Hylton 33, Robert Killington 35, Ernest Rose 19, William Thompson 32, Stephen Frederick Tunmore 23, William Tunmore 20, john Lambert Ward 25 and Robert Wilson 41. Afterwards, the memorial committee, the Bishop, the clergy and parents of the fifteen men were entertained to tea in the Parish Room by Mrs Flower Holmes of Strumpshaw Hall.

There was one happy footnote to the war. Alice Manthorpe, Strumpshaw's postwoman, who would have wed Frederick Tunmore, married Reginald Bunn, Burlingham's blacksmith who had survived the battle.

The war memorial after its unveiling in February 1920.

Chapter 22

◇

A Second War and Beyond

The victory of the Great War was followed by hard times and suffering. For most of the period in what is often labelled, 'between the wars' Strumpshaw folk were unprepared for another conflict. England had put its faith in the League of Nations, set up to settle quarrels by peaceful discussion.

But trouble flared in the 1930's. When Japan attacked China, and Mussolini, the Italian dictator, invaded Abyssinia, wartime would involve Strumpshaw once more. Czechoslovakia, Neville Chamberlain, Adolph Hitler, Poland and Winston Churchill were headline names which preceded the declaration of war with Germany, on 4 September 1939.

An immediate effect of the conflict was the silencing of the church bells. A national directive was that church bells would be used to sound the alert of an invasion so for the duration of the hostilities the three bells in St Peter's tower were not rung.

Percy Feek, Strumpshaw's sporting legend and reservist with the 2nd Battalion Norfolk Regiment was amongst the first to be called for service in 1939. But his regiment's incursion into France led to capture in July 1940 and imprisonment for a miserable five years at Marienburg, in the infamous Camp 20B, near East Prussia.

Arthur Grint was one of Strumpshaw's first conscripts of the Second World War. Lingwood born, he came to the village at three years old when his family took up residence in the new council house at 3 Buckenham Road in 1922. Barney, his father, had seen naval service on a minesweeper during the Great War having been a sailor on drifters in peacetime so war was no newcomer to the Grint family.

Arthur joined the Norfolk Regiment in November 1939 and after initial training went to France in the

A pre-war meeting of village heroes. Left to right: George Ashley, Matthew Coady and Arthur Grint, C1935.

April of 1940 as part of the British Expeditionary Force. He was an infantryman then and his unit had been sent to guard an important fuel storage. Soon after arrival the German armies broke through the Maginot Line. This was a series of defences built along the eastern border of France to hold back the enemy but the German forces had also entered France through Belgium and Holland. The episode lead to the famous evacuation of Dunkirk. The evacuation was completed before Arthur Grint's own unit returned to England:

'We were mobile and went up to Cherboug. We didn't know anything about Dunkirk as we were further inland. They loaded us up and we went through the peninsular where Cherboug is and home from there. We were among the last to come out I would say. It must have been June because it was my mother's birthday and I sent her a card as soon as we got back to England. I thought the war was over'

The war was really only beginning and Arthur Grint was safely home. The evacuation from the beaches of Dunkirk is still hailed as a miracle: 337,130 British and French troops were rescued from the beaches with the aid of over a thousand ships. The sea had never been so calm as an armada of 'little ships', some from neighbouring Brundall, were sent to ferry the retreating soldiers from the shore to waiting ships.

But one Strumpshaw boy never came back. He was Alfred Waterton a private in the 2nd Battalion Royal Norfolk Regiment, who died aged 29 on 24 May 1940, the village's first casualty of the war. He was the son of Albert and Ada Waterton who lived in The Loke and is commemorated on the Dunkirk Memorial.

Strumpshaw soon learned that this second 'hostility' was a different war. Twenty years on since 1918, the enemy could come visiting from the skies so at night a total blackout was enforced. No lights were allowed to be seen after dark. Most houses had thick, dark curtains covering the insides of windows and doors or a frame of light-proof material was put against each window. The local air raid warden would tour the village each evening to make sure no lights were showing all in the effort to prevent Strumpshaw being seen by enemy aircraft flying above. At this time the Goat public house (now Huntsman) was licensed to Alfred Brighton. He was designated the local air raid warden as son Ted recalled:

'John Watson at Lingwood was the head warden and he was supposed to get in his car and come down to alert the other wardens. My father became the warden because he couldn't be in the Home Guard as he'd been injured in the first war. That's why we took the pub. Watson roared to a halt on the Goat plain shouting "Air Raid!" My father who was out mowing the bowling green with his straw hat on and shorts and was supposed to get on his bike and ride all the way round Strumpshaw, blowing a whistle. Anyhow, my father jumped on his bike and set out blowing his whistle, blowing like hell and got as far as The Mutton and that was it. He eventually came rolling home at tea time! Jerry would have been over and bombed us to hell and gone home again. That was at the beginning of the war when nobody knew anything really'

Those heeding Alfred Brighton's warning would make for their air raid shelters. On the green opposite the school, an underground communal refuge had been built with the help of Cecil Curtis for the residents at that corner of the village. The school had its own shelter and next door to the Shoulder of Mutton, the Rose family built an Anderson (type of shelter) into the parting hedge.

But the village was soon put in the front line of defence. In the pasture now occupied by Strumpshaw Riding School a searchlight camp was established. A few buildings were erected; cookhouse, canteen, office and three large huts to house the soldiers. The cookhouse and living quarters were place along the field's edge under large oak trees to afford some camouflage. Emplacements were built to take the searchlight and gun-posts, listening device and electricity generator. The site was managed by ten soldiers with an officer who were members of the Welsh Fusiliers.

The object of the site was to listen for approaching enemy aircraft and sweep the sky with the powerful light to illuminate the target for the anti aircraft gunners to shoot down the aeroplanes, after correctly identifying it as enemy! There were other gun emplacements in surrounding villages such as Stokesby; carefully placed to intercept the enemy coming in from over the marshes from the North Sea on their way to Norwich. Strumpshaw's strategic high land, 130ft above sea level, once more was an asset. Every time the light was turned on the whole village seemed to be alight.

The Welsh Fusiliers sent to guard the searchlight installation were based in Brundall Gardens. Amongst their number was 19 year old Doug Jones: the furthest he had ever been from his home in Llanberis, North Wales. Catching his eye while he took duty at Brundall Gardens Halt was a vibrant young lady from Strumpshaw, Heather Rudd who lived in Buckenham Road, opposite the searchlight site. Doug's duties took in the area from Brundall, Reedham, Gt Yarmouth and back to Strumpshaw, guarding sensitive sites. But regimental duties allowed time to fall in love and Doug married Heather in Strumpshaw Church. Also in Buckenham Road at number seven lived the Stone family where son David was enjoying all that was now going on at the searchlight site:

'Entrance to the camp was directly opposite our house. A guard was on duty at all times although did nothing to prevent the kids going into the canteen to buy chocolate and sweets when they had been delivered, usually once a week. Directly opposite the canteen was the officer quarters and at this time Lieutenant Giles was in command. One afternoon during a very strong wind the entire roof blew off his hut. We were playing in the road at the time. It was very scary. During one air raid three bombs were dropped on the camp but luckily there were no injuries. I had slept through it and hadn't heard a thing.'

Also witnessing the war was ten year old Daphne Smith. Her grandfather, Frederick Kemp, was Strumpshaw's miller in 1896 but Daphne was born in London through her mother working there as a First World War nurse. At the peak of hostilities young Daphne was back in Strumpshaw living at the junction of Pack Lane and Chapel Road and could vividly recall an air raid:

'One night there were aeroplanes about and I just happened to be outside with my father and Fred

Strumpshaw as seen by the RAF aerial survey in July 1946. Long Lane winds through the top of the picture and some of the cornfields have been harvested. On the far right, halfway down, is the gravel working and to its left, the field showing light patches was the site of the searchlight platoon during the second war. (PICTURE, COURTESY OF NORFOLK MUSEUMS AND ARCHAEOLOGY SERVICE)

Guards of the Welsh Fusileers with Doug Jones in front row, far right.

Arthur Grint's garage in 2007. It was once part of the cookhouse at the searchlight site during World War II.

Dingle. They were standing on the green at the end of the lane. The searchlight beam caught a plane in the sky which dropped some flares. That happened to be a German and of course, fighters came after him. Anyway, there was some fighting going on and my mother and father shouted, "Get into the ditch, get into the ditch" and there was this ditch, full of water, "Get Down, get down, put your head down" and you could hear the shells rattling in the road. When it eased off a little bit he dropped what we called "bread baskets", all full of incendiaries and they fell in the orchard were there were chickens and geese and they were kicking up a heck of a row. There was my mother and other people trying to put the fires out'

Harvest time tea on Hollies Farm, 1939: Alice Church, Jimmy Turner, Wilfred Church, ?, Alfred Church.

During the war food was rationed. The population had been issued with ration books early in the hostilities which contained coupons for redeeming when purchasing food. With the village being a farming community it was technically self sufficient but officially everything had to be accounted for the national pot. During harvest time, and with rationing in place, the farm-workers could apply for extra rations like butter and sugar. Their work was deemed essential.

Strumpshaw's Hollies Farm, then owned by Alfred Church, contributed its share to the food supplies. But work was hindered by a shortage of men and son Wilfred was away serving in the army. To help keep Hollies in going order Alfred's daughter Elsie answered the national call to arms and joined the Women's Land Army.

Elsie had left school at 14 in 1936 to work in the comfort of the haberdashery department at Jarrold's in Norwich. At the start of the war she was driving the farm's first tractor and applying herself to the labours normally done by the men, carrying them through to peace time.

Even in this time of austerity normal life went on. Elsie Church met and married Ronald Roberts who was serving with the Royal Norfolk Regiment while he was stationed at the Britannia Barracks in Norwich. Elsie's bridesmaid was Dorothy Cox from Lingwood, another Land Army girl who married Arthur Grint in 1956.

Terry Atkins will always remember wartime Strumpshaw. His father Richard, who had survived the Great War, was in the Home Guard along with Bob Rowland, Bob Ashley and David Stone's father. For them it was like being in a part time army. At the beginning they carried out their patrols at night with pitch forks and sticks, but eventually everyone was given a uniform and rifle. Their purpose was to patrol the local area in case the Germans invaded and

Elsie Church as a Land Army girl with her brother Wilfred, c1940.

to help the Army and Police when required including duty on Strumpshaw's searchlight site. The very thought of men armed with sticks and pitchforks raises many a smile these days but at the time, propaganda had led the enemy to believe that a resistance movement was guarding England's shores.

Getting prepared in Strumpshaw was 14 Platoon, 4 Company, 6 Battalion Home Guard. The thirty strong group comprised of men from Lingwood, Strumpshaw, and Burlingham. Amongst their number was 40 year old Donald 'Mac' Walker whose son Peter spent some time in wartime Strumpshaw:

'This platoon carried out much of their training, gunnery and bayonet practice in the Strumpshaw gravel pits. My father, who was a lance corporal, used to bring home a bren machine gun with ammunition and keep it in the garden shed. Imagine that being allowed today. Some of the older men had

Above: *Wedding of Elsie Church and Ronald Roberts. Left to right: George Steward, Gwendolyn Roberts, Nellie Roberts, Ronald Roberts, Elsie, Alice Church, Dorothy Cox, William Roberts, Alfred Church.*

Right: *Dorothy Cox in the uniform of the Women's Land Army.*

In the years when our Country was in mortal danger

HARRY GEOFFREY TURNER

who served 21 June 1940 – 31 December 1944 gave generously of his time and powers to make himself ready for her defence by force of arms and with his life if need be.

George R.I.

THE HOME GUARD

Harry Turner's Home Guard certificate.

The Home Guard at Lingwood 1943. Left to right, back row: Tom Nichols, Douglas Adams, Victor Harper, John Simpson, Charlie Brown, Guy Nichols, Jim Knights, Bertie Nichols. Middle: Leonard Harper, Jack Stone, Ebon Mayes, ? Sutheland, Harry Turner, Bob Adams, ? Dye, Fred Tubby. Front: ?, Cecil Tree, Fred Hubbard, Mac Walker, Basil Groves, ? Rocke, Percy Cross, Michael Falcon, Sid Fisher, Bob Ashley, Frank Hall, Bob Mallett, Jim Portom, ?. (PICTURE BY COURTESY OF PETER WALKER)

served in the First World War and a few of the young men eventually had to fight in WW2. My father had served in the Cavalry from 1922-5'

Strumpshaw did receive some hefty lumps from on high. The searchlight site attracted, inevitably, some attention and authorities record that the first bombs to fall anywhere near Norwich came down here. On Sunday 2 June 1940 several districts in East Anglia were under a 'yellow warning'. These were due to returning British aeroplanes, one of which dropped two high explosive bombs near Strumpshaw's searchlight site, wounding one man and damaging telegraph wires. Dudley Rowland, Fred Rope and other pals cycled up to Stone Road where the bombs had dropped in the field opposite the current entrance to the Recycling Centre. The boys went in search of souvenir pieces of shrapnel, prised from the bark of an old oak tree which had taken the brunt of the explosion.

Tom Purdy at the Boxing Day shoot, 1983. The depression in the field, some distance away, is the crater caused by bombs which fell there during World War II.

On occasions day was indistinguishable from night. Searchlights swept the skies from Strumpshaw's hill and similar sites and the fires from air raids on Norwich and Great Yarmouth caused a vast glow in the skies. The village seemed caught in an arc of light projecting from the two towns. There was forever the sound of aircraft, the enemy's and our own; flying out and returning from raids and gunfire as batteries of anti-aircraft opened up a fusillade on the enemy planes, assisted by the light of the searchlight.

Strumpshaw's own hill was well alight in the early hours of one morning when the house of Mr Newruck was hit by incendiary bombs. The thatched roof was totally lost never to be replaced along with an upper

storey which was never rebuilt. Heather Rudd had dashed up to see the site and met up with her husband to be, Doug Jones, who had come over from searchlight duties. Heather recalled "I remember us walking up there and the bullets were flying around"

As the war intensified in 1941, the Parish Council convened an emergency meeting. The rector, Rev Wright chaired the gathering having invited the local police representative, Sergeant Payne, to outline the organising of resources in the event of a serious situation. Food supplies and a survey of the livestock would be handled by the Rev Wright; milk, Mr Childs; casualties would be dealt with by Mrs Twiss at the Hollies with severe cases being referred to the Red Cross in Norwich. Miss Day elected Billeting Officer, refugees going to the Union Workhouse at Lingwood for 48 hours before being billeted out. Air Raid Precautions were now reorganised under Herbert Mayes, the builder and undertaker. He would deal with victims needing decontamination; passing them to a centre in Thorpe and Burlingham. Mr Colman, the blacksmith, was nominated to deal with enemy activities and report to the military through the police. The village was prepared.

Far away from the home front, Strumpshaw's men were fighting in places they had barely heard of, in climates to which they were unaccustomed. Tunisia was the scene of a spectacular German retreat under Rommel, in the North Africa campaign, ahead of British and Allied troops. During this battle, Strumpshaw's second soldier was killed in action: Horace Forder, a gunner with the Royal Artillery in the 65th (The Norfolk Yeomanry) Anti-Tank Regiment, died Monday 22nd February 1943 at the age of 38. Left at home in Strumpshaw were his wife Olive and two sons, Ronald and Geoffrey.

The loss was devastating and Olive never fully recovered. By some consolation her parents George and Anna Tree were neighbours and stepped in to help raise their two grandsons. George was a hardened veteran of the first war and had lived to tell the tale of having his mount shot from under him. Horace Forder was laid to rest in the cemetery at Sfax and his widow died at the untimely age of 47.

In another ghastly corner of the world, Allied prisoners of war were being forced to work on the Burma-

Edna Cowles lived in Low Town and joined the National Fire Service c1942. Edna's brother Billy, was Squire Holmes' "boot boy" at the Hall.

Strumpshaw Red Cross Point, Chapel Road, 1945. Left to right: Hilda Rowland, Mrs Tipple, Mrs Dickson, Mrs Mingay.

Horace Forder, a Gunner with the Norfolk Yeomanry, who died in February 1943.

Arthur Grint, after Dunkirk.

Terry Atkins' cottage, saved from a flying bomb!

Siam railway. Strumpshaw's George Ashley had gone there as a driver with 251 Field Park Company, Royal Engineers but he died on 2nd September 1943. He is buried in the Chungkai War Cemetery, the site of the base camp where the prisoners had built a church and hospital. The war cemetery is the original burial ground, started by people like George Ashley, with the burials mostly for comrades who had died in the hospital.

Raising money for the war effort was ongoing. In Strumpshaw a dance was held every Friday night during the winter months in the large barn at The Hollies in Barn Hill. The event was supported by the public and military personnel stationed in the immediate area, Army, RAF, US Army and members of foreign squadrons serving in the RAF. A band of five or six players usually came from one of American bases. David Stone's father took care of the heating and cleaning for the event while his mother and other women baked cakes and made tea to be sold. But as always the threat from the skies was unforgettable as Terry Atkins recalled:

'I can remember a German coming over, machine gunning at a train, just over the unused railway bridge toward Lingwood and it came straight over our cottage here in Hemblington Rd. I remember a doodlebug (flying bomb) coming over here. Father shouted, "get under the table!", then it started up again. He said that it was the first one he'd ever heard start up'.

The flying bombs were launched rocket fashion from bases across the North Sea in Holland. The south of England was the intended target but a few went astray. The ghastly sound of the engine would be heard to cut out, signifying that the fuel had exhausted, causing it to plunge to earth and explode on impact. When the Atkins family heard the restarting engine they knew they were safe.

One morning in 1944 just as the Head-teacher, Mrs Buckton was taking prayers at the school, a doodle-bug did land nearby, and explode, beyond Brundall Station. She took the children out of school to the safety of the dug-out built by the parents in the field behind the school. One of the bars in the ornate window was cracked by the bomb's impact causing the ornately coloured glass to be lost.

Pte Harold William Struthers High who died in Singapore 21 September 1944.

Herbert Mayes, the local builder and his men repaired the window with plain glass, to be forever a reminder of war.

Also in 1944 plans were being laid to advance into Europe and force a way through to Germany. Arthur Grint was back in training for a return to France, to land on the beaches at Normandy, but nobody knew when:

'I was now part of the 1st Battalion and we started training for the invasion. We always knew it was going to happen. We did a lot of training up in Scotland, jumping off landing-craft in the lochs, getting so wet and marching so far; getting used to going over to Normandy. We should have gone on the 5 June from Newhaven but the weather was bad so we laid there for a couple of days. There were several dummy installations, ships, convoys, placed at readiness to fool the German photo reconnaissance so they weren't sure what was coming over to France'

Arthur had been given medical training for the invasion for his vital role as a stretcher bearer. The army medics had discovered his eyesight was poor which prevented him from more serious soldiering but he remained a devoted participant. The medical training was based mostly on the St John Ambulance teachings. As one of a team of four he carried a folding stretcher, a bag of shell dressings, triangular bandages and phials of pain killing drugs to administer intravenously. On 6 June D-Day came and the wait was over for what became known as 'the longest day'. Sword Beach was the destination for Arthur Grint's battalion as they crossed the English Channel and his only means of defence under fire was a red cross band on his arm:

'It was noisy and we were lucky really. We were on a landing craft called Infantry and there were about 120 men of the company aboard. The ramps went down, we jumped off and never got our feet wet; after all that training. The tide was just right. We got off the beach OK and waded through a field of flax. I'd never seen a field of flax before. We'd only just got inland a couple of miles, to a farmhouse, when somebody shouted "stretcher bearer!" I went forward to where a chap was wounded and got down against him when a mortar bomb exploded nearby and wounded me. I could walk but it surprised me when they said I would have to go back home. They didn't want wounded passengers out there'

Arthur Grint, on cycle, with colleagues pose by a "Croc", a flame throwing tank, somewhere in Germany c1944.

Percy Feek married Winifred Fox, at Strumpshaw, 1947.

Ronald Roberts, Royal Norfolk Regiment 1940-46.

Percy Feek with daughter Anne and a few of his trophies, c1950.

Back at the beach Arthur was loaded on to a DUKW (amphibious vehicle) and taken out to sea to board a ship which had just landed tanks and guns. The ship had been adapted for hospital use so he joined the injured and steamed back to England. After spending a night at a hospital, just inland, there was a coach trip to Yorkshire and another hospital for an operation to remove shrapnel.

While Arthur Grint was recovering, his Strumpshaw friend, Harold High, was in Singapore serving with the Bedford & Hertfordshire Regiment. He was the last of the village's servicemen to die, on 21 September 1944 and with no known grave is commemorated on the Singapore Memorial. Harold had come to Strumpshaw with his mother Beatrice, to live in one of the blacksmith's cottages, to keep house for Mr Springall. Harold was well known and liked and had formed a friendship with Dorothy Atkins the sister of Terry. The war had changed the course of another life.

Arthur Grint recovered and was intent on returning to duty. His old company, by now, had forged a way through to Holland:

'I joined them in Holland and went right through to the end of the war. I was still a stretcher bearer. We'd pick up those left behind who needed first aid. Attend to the badly wounded first, put splints on broken legs and assure them they'd be alright. You had to do it to keep their spirits up. There were four of us in the team and corporal. We picked up Germans as well, under the Geneva Convention. We didn't have any rifles, just the red cross armbands but we were still in the line of fire. We had jeeps to carry stretchers back to the regimental aid post, which were just tents with an operating theatre. During this time my mother wrote to say that a house in Strumpshaw had lost its chimney when struck by lightning. I had to smile because almost every house was bombed where we were!'

Thirty two conscripted men and ten women from the village were eventually drawn into World War II. They found themselves being despatched

Shepherd Goodwin, right of photograph, in Venice 1945.

Albert Mallett.

much further than their first war contemporaries, to places like North Africa, and the Far East, when Singapore and Hong Kong fell to the Japanese.

When the end of war came Strumpshaw's boys were spread throughout the world. Shepherd Goodwin was in Venice, the place these days many would just dream of being, but to him and his compatriots Italy had been no holiday. Some had suffered prison camps which would have lifelong effects and as in 1918, when all returned safely home, Strumpshaw and the world would never be the same.

In February 1946 Percy Feek was discharged having suffered five years imprisonment. On return to Strumpshaw he worked as a relay-man on the railway and married Winifred Fox in 1947. His celebrity status as an athlete saw him admired and he was called upon to open Lingwood fête although his running was now less ambitious. The wartime incarceration had taken a certain toll and Percy Feek died suddenly at work in February 1962 at the untimely age of 48. Percy's skill as a runner provided a glittering episode for his time in Strumpshaw, with trophies and medals now his epitaph.

When families had been reunited and the stories were told there were moves to record Strumpshaw's gratitude to those who had served. Firstly a roll of honour was hung in the church, to compliment the list from the First World War. Frank Futter of Oaklands Farm was a committee member and it was decreed that no ranks or ages be displayed. This was an early implementation of change from what had been customary. Those who served from Strumpshaw were:

'George Ashley, Richard Atkins, Charles Beck, Percy Blyth, Robert Carter, Wilfred Church, Irene Collins, Joseph Cunningham, George Draper, Ella Drew, Wilfred Etheridge, Arthur Forder, Edward Forder, Horace Forder, Victor Forder, William Forder, Percy Feek, Joseph Fox, Richard Fox, Frank Futter, Joyce Futter, Shepherd Goodwin, Arthur Grint, Harold High, Edna Key, David Lodge, Albert

Stonemason, Keith Pitt, adding the four names to Strumpshaw's war memorial in November 1982. (PICTURE BY COURTESY OF EASTERN DAILY PRESS)

The four names of the Second World War fallen are dedicated, 14 November 1982, by Canon Townsend.

Arthur Grint marries Dorothy Cox in 1956.

Alison Peart lays the Parish Council's wreath, 2003.

Arthur Grint, 2007.

Mallet, Grace Moy, Ronald Roberts, Fred Rope, Ivy Rose, Stanley Rose, Dudley Rowland, Robert Sargent, Maurice Saunders, Margaret Symonds, Pamela Symonds, Rosemary Symonds, Joan Turner, Frank Ward, Alfred Waterton, Edward Wooler, Arnold Youngs'

After the Great War and the institution of war memorials a Parliamentary act was passed to maintain the structures and plaques which had been put up by public subscription. Another act was introduced in 1947 whereby a local authority could add the names of the fallen from subsequent wars. Throughout England in cities, towns and villages an exhausted yet grateful populace implemented the provisions of the act and stone masons were set to work. But not in Strumpshaw.

On 24 May 1950 the parish council met to consider a request for the cleaning the war memorial at Buckenham and adding the name of its one casualty. After some discussion the council decided the rector should call a meeting to hear what parishioners and the British Legion would do, before taking any action.

As for Strumpshaw honouring its own recent war dead, nothing happened. Four men had given their all; four families had been left devastated. The relatives hoped for a memorial but were left drained of the clout to protest. There were living in the village, sons, grandchildren, a cousin and nephew of the fallen. The saddest indictment uttered at the time was the absence of an officer rank amongst the four who died. No doubt the family of an officer might have carried some sway.

Then a ray of hope came in 1957. A lady in the parish made moves to have the names added to the memorial and began to raise funds but to no avail. In March 1959 Buckenham War Memorial was on the agenda of the parish council again over concerns of its cleanliness but still no mention of Strumpshaw's absent fallen. The village had failed miserably.

Not until 1982 were the names finally added when a newly-elected

Gerald Fox (left) in Cyprus, 1953.

Terry Atkins in Malaya, 1959

parish councillor, Stephen Peart, urged the council to implement the provisions of the War Memorials Act. A handcrafted Cornish stone addition, bearing the names of the second war fallen, was added to the plinth of the Celtic cross in time for commemoration at the Armistice Sunday service in November 1982. From that date forever; George Ashley, Horace Forder, Harold High and Alfred Waterton, would be remembered.

But one old soldier always knew why he was there. Arthur Grint stood honourably, every year, remembering his friend Harold High who never came back. Arthur had been a supporter of getting the names added but was one of those people conditioned not to make too much fuss.

After the war, Arthur wanted to be a harness maker because he had 'done a bit of leather work in the army'. But horses were giving way to tractors so he took the offer of a job with an upholsterer in Norwich and another firm in Great Yarmouth. When that finished he joined Broom's Boatyard in Brundall and stayed for 22 years. In 1956 he married Dorothy Cox of Lingwood and they settled into the house where Arthur had lived since he was three years old. Arthur Grint died 19 August 2009 and his ashes were interred at Strumpshaw on 8 October.

Beyond the second war came preparation for future conflicts in the form of National Service. Men between the ages of 17 and 21 were expected to serve in the armed forces for eighteen months. Gerald Fox, brother-in-law of Percy Feek, went to Cyprus in 1953 and Terry Atkins travelled much further:

'I did my National Service in Malaya. I went there in 1959 and it was getting to the end of it then with the terrorists but you still had to carry a gun where ever you went. I was there twenty months, six weeks basic training and 3 or 4 weeks trade training. I came top of the thing so they gave me a choice of Germany or Malaya so I said "Malaya, please." I was given two days leave and sailed on Boxing Day. I'd love to go back'

Chapter 23

Round the Bend and into Lackford Run

The motto "Keep your bowels open and trust in the Lord" was that of a generation drawing close to extinction. "Eat your greens" lingers in the ears of many a Strumpshaw child whose parents worked a garden growing their own vegetables who in turn had been taught the need for roughage in their diet. Strumpshaw school pupils were taught the rudiments in Mrs Dann's gardening class in 1949. Even the smallest cottages in the parish had some form of garden.

Tucked away in one corner of all gardens was a little brick outhouse. Many had two doors, one for the coal store and the other for the lavatory. Inside, a wooden seat concealed a large galvanised receptacle, technically a pail closet, but to many, it was the 'thunder bucket'. For the children there was often a small version, by the side of the adult's seat.

As the average week progressed and a healthy life was lived by all, the bucket would need emptying. Up until the late 1940's this was a job for the man of the house and Dudley Rowland remembers one particular occasion being instructed by his father Bob:

'I used to get home before him and that was wintertime. He said when you get home tonight will you dig me a hole in the garden, which I did. Anyhow, father come home and had his tea and said "where is it?" I said "that's about so and so down the garden" so way go father, his rubber boots and a torch and the bucket and they were big old buckets. I don't know where he was shining the torch but he stepped in the hole! You can imagine it, can't you? The bucket tipped up, his boots were full and of course we had no bathroom so he had to wash outside!'

This weekly routine for most households was alleviated when the Rural District Council started

the night soil collection service. Within living memory the chaps on the "honey cart" were George Payne and Sheila Greenfield's father. Night soil was the polite way of dealing with the unmentionable but problems arose when the collectors paid earlier calls. In June 1948 Herbert Mayes, Strumpshaw's builder, undertaker and Parish Councillor reported to a council meeting that:

'The RDC officials were collecting night soil from the houses in the parish in the daytime, also at Buckenham and Hassingham and it was proposed by Mr Rope and seconded by Mr Mayes that a letter of protest be sent to the RDC to discontinue the practice.'

But the unmentionable seemed to be unspeakable. In Strumpshaw there was no night soil collection because George Payne and his father before him had to deal with the stuff; in the daytime. Their council brief was to empty the pails of a sizeable population and they did it for twenty years. There was 'health and safety' advice for the operators: hold breath, lift bucket to top of the lorry's tank, turn head away and splosh! Protective clothing and boots were supplied along with a large can of disinfectant for use at the end of the day.

Once the pail closets had been emptied the cart would disgorge its load. Strumpshaw's depository was in Cuckoo Lane all over the fields of Tom Hewitt

Noel Hewitt of High Noon Farm, 2009.

at High Noon Farm. For Tom's son Noel the procedure was second nature:

'We always had the emptying up here. There was George Payne and a chap named Easter, they were the regular two, just a little Bedford lorry with a flat tank on the back. They used to come up and drive up the field and old Easter at the back would hit the lever and the old boy would drive

Mrs Dann's gardening class at Strumpshaw School, c1949. Left to right: Raymond Broom, Gerald Woolston, Noel Hewitt, Evelyn Knights, Mrs Dann, Tony Bartram, ?, Raymond Driver, Brenda Beck, Janet Cunningham, Gillian Calver, Madeline Rose, ?.

Dudley Rowland's family. Left to right, back: Bob Rowland (father), Bob Rowland (grandfather). Front: Dudley, Grandmother with Brian Rowland on lap, Bob Rowland (brother).

A privy, (lavatory) somewhere near Strumpshaw, sitting it out in 2009!

up the field in rows. Just over the bridge, in Cuckoo Lane, there was a big low in the bit of land and father used to let them back up there when they couldn't get on the land, like in wintertime and tip it in there. We then hulled some straw on top; muck it out once a year and spread it. It was mainly for the sugar beet so we had sugar beet so high you could just about wade through it'

It was organic farming in the truest sense although local advice was to avoid the area for a day or so, especially in the hot weather. Even when the sewerage treatment plant opened next door to High Noon Farm and most folk were connected to mains drainage, Tom Hewitt was still on the receiving end. The treatment process produced some solid by-product and this was placed into two rotary muck-spreaders parked conveniently near the works. Noel would get a call to say they were full so they were brought up to the pastures or fields for spreading. But legislation brought the operation to a close when it was considered the stuff going on to the land was unfit, organically, with all the products being flushed down parish plugholes.

Despite the age of modern domestics, disposing of wet waste was an issue as recent as January 1977. A tipping-pit by Buckenham Woods was used by Broadland District Council to take the contents of cesspools, septic tanks and remaining pail closets and the authority wanted to continue with increased discharge. Strumpshaw Parish Council recommended refusal.

The communal water pump for Buckenham Road's council houses, in Arthur Grint's front garden, 2007.

For a continued healthy life natural bodily functions relied on ablutions. In the days before piped mains the village drew its water from an abundance of wells. There was a well within reach of each group of houses, with rights to draw water often written into the deeds. Terry Atkins who lives in the cottage where he was born, in Hemblington Road, remembers getting water from the well next door at The Cedars. His family also had their own well in the driveway between them and the other neighbours and as Terry recalled, "many times I've dropped a pail down there!"

Water became a highlight of Arthur Grint's life when as a child of three years, his family took up residence a 3 Buckenham Road in 1921. Their garden housed the communal well with a hand-pump which served the row of new council houses. Everybody came to the front garden to pump water from the 46ft deep well. During the second war the council installed an artisan pump to lift the water to a 40 gallon tank, with a pipe to a tap toward the middle of the houses. As residents drew their water from the supply, pressure dropped and the pump would start to refill the tank.

The larger houses in the village, like Strumpshaw Hall and the Hollies, had ventured into plumbing. The water was drawn from below ground with the aid of sophisticated machinery, helped by a donkey, as Billy Cowles recalled:

'All the water at the Barnes' house was pumped by

Above: *Kathy Mills' Morris 8 car and Turner family picnic.*

Right: *Kathy Mills at Little Orchard, The Loke c1980.*

donkey. They had the circular walk round. They'd put him in and set him off and he'd be going round there half the day, nobody with him. He drew the water up to get it into the house. At the hall it used to be pumped by hand. My father did it for a long time. He used to go up at night, for extra money, and fill the tanks up and they would last all day'

Ann Turner recalled the precious commodity of water. The Turner family lived at Hill Rise where they had resided since leaving Oaklands:

'Saturday was bath night. Aunt Kathy used to go first and then everyone else followed; in the same water, lovely and scummy by the time it got to Susie. Hair wash was once or twice a week; you could not complain, you dare not complain. Mondays was always washdays. The night before dad would have laid the fire underneath the copper water boiler in the scullery. The fire used to burn any old boxes, shoes, slippers, margarine papers; anything that would burn. Mum would spend most of Monday morning washing and rinsing everything out by hand. There was no washing machine or spin dryer so everything had to be mangled. Whatever the weather, provided it was dry, whether it was cold and frosty the washing still went out. Lines full, all over the garden at Hill Rise'

Water quality was an issue for new babies. When Jean Beardwood was born at the council houses in Buckenham Road her parents' had their own well but at her birth the water quality was considered unsuitable. Instead, the water given to Jean was drawn from the well of 'Drover' Church at Hillcrest in Barn Hill.

In the mid 1950's Strumpshaw took a step toward modern times when piped water was laid. A pumping station was built at the marsh end of Low Town along with two modern cottages for occupation by the works' attendants. Two bores drew water from the ground at 50 litres a second and filtered it before pumping it to an underground reservoir, built on the top of Mill Hill. From there it supplied, by gravity, much of the area, including Strumpshaw. Demand eventually called for a third bore.

The original water supply had been a complex operation for a small village. Mains were laid along the roads with branches to each property terminating at a stop valve from which the residents organised a plumber to connect into their house. Overseeing this operation was the Water Inspector, a newly married Arthur Marriot from Norwich who brought his wife Rita to occupy one of the Waterworks Cottages in

Neville Burton and Arthur Marriot thawing frozen pipes during the freeze of 1963.

1950; "miles from anywhere and one bus a week!" The weekly rent was £1, deducted from his wages, "which left about a tenner!"

Strumpshaw was now washing at the turn of a tap and even flushing. Some enterprising households had taken advantage of installing WC's, draining to their own septic tanks. The days of the night cart appeared to be numbered.

In the mid 1990's the water was noticeably hard with its iron content and a saline presence. The original pumping station was beginning to work under strain so the authority's answer was to pipe the supply from the Mousehold reservoir in Norwich. A major civil engineering undertaking extended a pipeline through fields and under roads to the reservoir on Mill Hill. Strumpshaw's hill top reserve supplies a population zone of more than 15000 people, taking in Acle, Beighton, Blofield, Cantley, Horning, Reedham, Upton, Woodbastwick as well as our village.

The coming of mains water meant the ultimate luxury of mains drainage and the flushing loo, not to mention a real bath. But mains drainage called for a modern disposal system so Strumpshaw's first sewerage treatment plant was built in 1964 by the boundary with Brundall. It was situated conveniently by the Lackford Run, a clear stream able to receive the final effluent from the plant before it flowed through to the River Yare.

The mammoth task of building the works and digging up the roads once more, brought Strumpshaw another step into the modern age. The contractor was Andrews of Leeds and amongst their staff was Kenny Wilkins of Strumpshaw. After seeing through the project he moved on elsewhere for two years then returned to see out the life of the works.

By 1969 the Blofield & Flegg Rural District Council were aware the treatment plant was becoming over-

The sewerage treatment plant in 1983.

Fishing in the Lackford Run. Left to right: Tom London, Freddie Carver and Ben London.

loaded. The system had to cope with the expansion of Lingwood as more houses were built and added to the flow. The solution was a large extension.

The enlarged works opened on 17 October 1973 at a cost of £420,000 one of the largest of its kind built in Norfolk after the Second World War. The new scheme boasted pioneering features in the form of plastic filters and an aerobic digester for the treatment of sludge.

The works was a haven for wildlife. The fellows who kept the place in going order could tell exactly when the first swallows arrived, when the first cuckoo was heard and how many wagtails had been seen that year. There was a gentleness about the place, a quietness disturbed only by quarrelsome starlings fighting over the best pickings around one of the vast settling tanks.

The operation never stopped. Pumping stations in Blofield, Brundall, Lingwood and Strumpshaw conveyed the effluent from each neighbourhood by the pumps being switched automatically as the flow dictated. The system was designed to handle almost two and a half million gallons a day. Indicators in a control room showed what was happening miles distant, in places like Acle Road, Lingwood or Hemblington Road, Strumpshaw.

The flushings of the four villages arrived at Strumpshaw through the inlet works. Everything then passed through a screening process to trap the things that should not have been flushed round the bend. Stubborn properties which defied liquidising, like children's toys, razor blades, hair pins, cotton buds and the abundance of latex rubber, were manually removed.

The liquid passing through the system arrived at circular filter beds. A mass of slag, like

Harry Rose c1945.

the ballast used under railway tracks was constantly trickled with liquid effluent from sweeping, revolving arms, to find its way to the bottom, emerging as fairly clear water. At the end of the process a crystal clear liquid was adding to the flow of the Lackford Run, passing under the bridge, where village boys with rods and lines patiently waited for a bite.

Eventually, Strumpshaw's modern piece of civil engineering was outmoded. The works closed and the flushings of a vastly increased population was rerouted to the treatment plant at Whitlingham.

The Lackford Run in 2010 has returned to a natural stream. Long before piped water and mains drainage it was a wide dyke draining large areas of Braydeston meadowland where it was forded by an old trail, winding its way from Pack Lane. The source of The Run was far beyond Blofield at Harker's Lake and had been a deep wide stream, managed by Harry Rose, the local marshman. In his young days it was ten feet deep in parts and full of fish, with a wind-pump which drew water from the marshes and returned it to the stream. The river walls were banked and flood-doors, worked by the pressure of water, controlled the tides; by opening when the level went down and closing when the tides rose.

Before the second war The Lackford Run was silted with mud and almost bare at low tide. There was no trace of the wind-pump and the flood doors were broken. Harry Rose, christened Henry and known throughout his life as Dueshie, could be seen cleaning out one remaining dyke on a marsh where cattle were being fed and he once remarked: "Nothing's like it used to be. Even the beer isn't the same"

◇

Chapter 24

Front Line Strumpshaw

In September 1803, when England was threatened with invasion from France, a telegraph was installed on Strumpshaw mill. By semaphoric means, messages would be received from Norwich Castle, relayed to Filby church and thence to Great Yarmouth. At this time in history, semaphore signals were the fastest means of communication. Strumpshaw was sitting on very high ground and France's Napoleon Bonaparte was in the middle of a quarrel with England, boastfully declaring that he would invade the country.

In October, the Norfolk and Norwich Volunteer Regiments took on permanent duty in Great Yarmouth and needed to know when the French were coming. Any warnings of the invasion would be sent via Strumpshaw. In the event, Nelson scattered the French fleet at Trafalgar in 1805, and so held off Bonaparte for the time being.

In the meantime, the threat remained serious. Experiments with a new telegraph system had started in 1795, invented by Revd Lord George Murray, to link London and the south coast ports. An extension of the system to Great Yarmouth included Strumpshaw as part of a chain of telegraph stations. All traces of the telegraph have long gone but Strumpshaw's Hilary Hammond captured that illustrious period from the village's past:

Hilary Hammond, close to the site of the Shutter Telegraph station.

'In 1808 the Admiral in Great Yarmouth sent the first message to the Admiralty in London using the newly installed shutter telegraph system. This was, briefly, "Calypso ready for sea". It would have taken about 17 minutes for this signal to reach London. HMS Calypso was a brig used mainly to escort convoys.*

The signalling system was based on a grid of six large shutters that could be seen from up to 12 miles away. These could either be open or closed, so that the 63 different combinations spelled out letters, words and numbers.

The new telegraph was needed because the Admiralty had based a large fleet at Great Yarmouth. This operated in the North Sea and the Baltic to respond to the threat posed by the French and their Russian allies during the Napoleonic wars. Prior to this system being built, the only way information could be passed from Great Yarmouth to London was by sending messages via stage coach, or a boat along the East coast, both of which took a day or so each way.

The obvious route was to take the messages up what is now the line of the A12, but the surveyor, George Roebuck, was concerned that the smoke from London and the amount of fog in Essex would mean that messages often would not be able to be passed. Thus he decided to use relatively high ground and take the line out of London to St. Albans, and then via the Dunstable Downs, along the Chilterns and the Gog Magog hills to Great Yarmouth via Newmarket, East Harling, Carleton Rode, Wreningham, Norwich, and Strumpshaw.

Each station was between 7 and 12 miles away from the next. The station in Norwich was based on what is now Telegraph Hill, while that at Strumpshaw was near the windmill, on Mill Hill. Strumpshaw is the highest ground between Norwich and Great Yarmouth. Each telegraph station had a crew of 3 or 4: one or two with telescopes to look at the adjacent telegraph stations, and two to operate the shutters through a system of ropes and pulleys. The signals were sent using normal language, but with shortened words, rather like texting today. The message was then sent using combinations of shutter positions until it ended, when all the shutters were set to "open" to show the end of the signal.

Some of the log books from the Gog Magog station have survived, and are kept at the National Maritime Museum in Greenwich. The records show that the longest signal for the period covered took 29 minutes to send, while the shortest took 2 minutes, with an average of 17 minutes per signal.

The telegraph was used to send short messages only: detailed dispatches were still sent by road. The whole system did not survive the cuts made after the end of the Napoleonic wars. All the stations were sold off at the end of 1814, and there are very few, if any, indications on the ground today showing where the stations stood'

The Royal Observer Corps (ROC), underground at Strumpshaw, during an exercise in 1966.

Strumpshaw was an intermediate station. It was manned by at least three men, a midshipman and two assistants, to operate the shutters and telescopes. They kept watch every five minutes but could not operate at night.

The Shutter Telegraph might seem impossibly primitive for today's generations. But 150 years later with improved technology, a threat far worse than Napoleon placed the village on a very different map of communications.

A Royal Observer Corps member charges the Ground Zero Indicator during an exercise.

The period of 1945-1991 is recognised as the Cold War. World powers were in political conflict, there was military tension; economic competition and forever a threat of nuclear war. In the event of such a conflict, East Anglia, it was reckoned, would be an early target through the presence of American military bases. The defence on the ground amounted to a system of monitoring posts to assess the outcome and enable the direction of resources. This is where Strumpshaw was put on the map.

Norfolk was covered by fifty five underground measuring posts in clusters of three, four and five. These would be manned by the Royal Observer Corps (ROC) as a continuance of their role in the second war. The map shows Brundall in a cluster with Coltishall and Hellesdon, a triangle covering Norwich, but for Brundall we must read Strumpshaw. At the ROC control centre at Chartwell Road in Norwich the large map on its wall clearly stated Strumpshaw. Brundall had been the ROC post in World War 2 but was removed as post war development encroached on the site. Strumpshaw's bunker, a master post, was built in the middle of high and open ground at Tom Hewitt's High Noon Farm in June 1961.

If a nuclear attack was imminent the bunkers all over the county would have been occupied immedi-

ately by three ROC members. They would descend into their concrete underground fortress equipped with various measuring devices linked to ground level, bunk beds, food and water, a car battery for power, telephone, radio and a chemical toilet, to wait for the attack. A Bomb Power Indicator, a pressure device, would measure the force of the atomic explosion while a Ground Zero Indicator, a four-way pin-hole camera, pointing north, south, east and west would record the flash of the bomb. The operator would have to wait for the outside conditions to become safe before emerging to examine the pin-hole camera. Along with results from a device to measure radioactive fallout each bunker in the county would pass its findings to the central control room in Norwich. From there a pattern would emerge as to the effect of the attack and tell the necessary authorities how and where to deal with survivors. During those years of Cold War threat regular exercises were held, yet very few people, outside, were aware of their presence.

In 1968 a restructuring retained twenty four of the original posts. Strumpshaw was then linked in a new cluster to Honingham, Hellesdon and Stalham. National exercises were held twice a year for eight hours on a Sunday. Once a year, international exercises involved the linking up with warning and monitoring groups throughout Europe. Observers from each cluster met once a month and individual post meetings took place 39 times in a year. The purpose was to test the equipment and phone lines or just general post maintenance.

In 1991 the Home Office and Ministry of Defence decided the ROC would end active training. Technology and the changes in world politics brought and end to one of the cheapest and most committed voluntary organisations. Strumpshaw's bunker, like many others, was closed and eventually put to public tender. A cellular telephone operator was interested because of the site's strategic position on high ground but getting power laid on proved difficult. Noel Hewitt, on whose land the bunker was built put in a bid but eventually it was sold to an outside buyer in 2003.

◇

Chapter 25

The New Generations

On 17 March 1967 the Eastern Daily Press carried a headline proclaiming Strumpshaw was a dying village. The revelation followed a public inquiry at Acle to consider appeals against planning refusals for two plots on Norwich Road, east of The Loke. A Norwich estate agent pressed the case by suggesting that more houses would introduce new families but the Ministry of Housing and Local Government inspector ruled: "Strumpshaw was not considered suitable for expansion."

The disappointed agent who prophesied the village's decease was proved wrong. An epitaph was never written and in due course someone else built the houses. Strumpshaw has been kept alive by people who desired to live here, mostly by design, because they love the way the village breathes.

If there is a heaven's eye view of the village then Mike Page has photographed it. No one more than him has witnessed Strumpshaw's changing land-scape and seasons since the Royal Air Force made its aerial survey in 1946. The post war photo reconnais-sance was commissioned to assist the country's future planning.

These days, an aerial photograph of Norfolk appearing in the local newspaper is likely to carry Mike Page's credit. He started flying a De Havilland Tiger Moth in 1960 and combined it with a love of taking pictures, nurtured in the school classroom at his native Gorleston. Those were the days of black and white film being processed in a 'dark room under the stairs.'

Mike came to Strumpshaw in 1973 to establish his motor repair business on the Norwich Road site once occupied by the threshing contractor, Sam Howes.

Strumpshaw c.1980 showing gravel working landfill site, bottom of picture, centre.

PHOTO BY MIKE PAGE

Together with his wife Gillian they built and expanded the operation, added workshops, took on body repairs and motorcycles and became a registered MOT centre. In between times Mike would get airborne from Seething Airfield and gradually established an impressive library of aerial views. Then came a revolution; digital photography and a new discipline in picture taking:

Mike Page and Cessna, 2009.

'I always use a co-pilot who flies my Cessna aircraft while I concentrate on composing and capturing the image. The cameras are hand-held and pictures are taken with the windows open! I use shutter speeds of between 1/200 and 1/2000 of a second depending on the amount of turbulence.

Flying at around 90-100 miles per hour over the subject and taking pictures all the time leads me to use the phrase 'slight differences make all the difference'. Spring and summer, autumn and winter, sunlight and showers, my view of the landscape from above is forever changing in colour and texture. I can never capture the exact same image again.'

From above, Mike sees Strumpshaw's three distinct communities; Low Town, the higher ground of the village along Norwich Road and Chapel Road. Thousands of images now fill his library and he supplies all manner of organisations, schools, general public and the media. The proceeds, along with royalties coming from his published books of aerial images, are donated to charity.

Further along the road, pictures of a very different kind are created by artist, Paula Fenton. Her speciality is pet portraiture which grew from the first commission, at the age of 16, into what is now a full-time profession. She had been drawing since a youngster but took a break from the art while working at Norwich Union.

Artist, Paula Fenton at work on a pastel of "Wesley".

Paula was born in Rotherham and came to Norfolk at the age of 14, "kicking and screaming" when her father took a business interest locally. She stayed for 'O' and 'A' levels then went back to Leeds University. When looking for a new home Paula and husband Paul were smitten with Strumpshaw after falling for one of the houses in Herbert Colman Close. Its atmosphere provides her inspiration to work from photographs, producing portraits in soft pastel which emphasize the animal's unique personality:

'I've never drawn a person and I think I would find it very difficult. People tell me I catch something of their animal, their pet, especially if they've lost it, which they don't get in photographs, so it is special. The work is mostly commissioned, quite a lot of local business. It's very nearly all dogs, a few horses and very odd cats, a couple of cows and a camel! The camel came from a photograph someone had taken in the Sudan during the 1970's. They wanted it painted. That was the strangest'

Another artist, Gloria Forster from Halvergate went to Norwich's Art School and met designer, David Fagg. After marriage, they set up house in Strumpshaw, where it was built for them in 1960 by Gloria's father, a master bricklayer. Gloria had been

"Wesley".

Paula Fenton, left, and Kiki Angelrath at Blofield's dog training class.

Gloria Fagg, 2009.

Roger Mayor.

Jan and Jim Saunt.

Kevin London with some of his 9000 day-old French Partridges.

Adam Hilburn with a handful of day-old partridges.

163

destined to follow in mother's footsteps, as a teacher of infants, but she never warmed to the profession. Instead, she shared in husband David's printing business when they traded as Martlet Studio, in their new house on the hill above the village.

The neighbouring Mill Hill, then a working quarry, and the ancient Buckenham Woods, nearby, was always Strumpshaw to Gloria. The house may have been remote from the village but the inspiration to sketch was all around. When the gravel working became redundant, nature took control and wild flowers appeared. There was always a piece of abandoned machinery, derelict pumps and mills on the fen, let alone the pubs and the church. Gloria amassed a portfolio which bore testimony to a Strumpshaw of gentler days.

The attraction of that same hill drew Roger Mayor from Buckinghamshire. Desiring a new life, mid term, he was already nurturing a soft spot for Norfolk having owned a boat on the Broads for a number of years. By the time he came to Strumpshaw as a resident in 2002, a move that coincided with his marriage to Penny, Roger was a well established composer, arranger and record producer.

One of his musical works with a strong Norfolk connection is The Julian Oratorio, with text written by the 14th Century mystic, Julian of Norwich. This full scale choral piece, the first serious work to set her words to music, was composed after Roger came to live in Norfolk. Other works with a strong local connection include his album 'Watercolours' for solo piano, inspired by coastal and country scenes around Norfolk and Suffolk.

Roger and Penny were married in Strumpshaw church and set up home in Barn Hill which provided the privacy and quietness needed by a composer and musician. The house boasted a dais-like level in the drawing room ideally suited for a Steinway piano.

Strumpshaw congregations first met Roger playing the keyboard for some of the church concerts to aid the roof appeal funds or at local Songs of Praise gatherings in the garden of the Old Rectory. For Roger and Penny the church is clearly the focus of the community in Strumpshaw and they are glad to be part of it.

Much of Roger's working life had been spent in and around London, initially teaching music in Edgeware then as a freelance arranger and producer working from home in the Chiltern Hills. Even here there was too much noise and too much traffic. Roger will always be thankful for being able to leave that behind for the tranquillity of the Norfolk countryside, living on the hill in Strumpshaw and overlooking the Fen.

From way down under came Jim and Jan Saunt. They met and married in Australia and worked in Kenya before coming to England in 1968. Jim spent 20 years with Outspan, the importers of citrus fruit, which led to his book *Citrus Varieties of the World: an Illustrated Guide* being hailed as a leading authoritative work.

In 1990, Jim and Jan moved into Plovers Hill at the top of Buckenham Road. The 18 century house was originally thatched and was home to the Pyle family, who owned the freehold of the mill at one time. More famously, in recent times, it was home to John Newruck, smallholder, shopkeeper, rabbit breeder, visiting grocery-man and one time undertaker. In those days it was known as The Laurels but was renamed by Tim and Gillian Harvey who took it on in a ruinous state after John Newruck died in 1965. They laid out its formal garden but subsequent owners allowed deterioration. Jim and Jan set out a recovery scheme once they became resident having first seen the place in 1988:

'We managed to buy it two years later when the garden was in need of tender care, with saplings growing out of the yew hedge and molehills covering the lawn. Most of the original shrubs have gone but the replacements are now approaching full maturity. The orangery, a wholly glass structure, designed by our daughter Deborah and David Hills of DSDHA Architects was erected in 1999 and won a regional RIBA award in the Building of the Year Award of 2000. This feature of the house and garden brought a great deal of attention into our lives with articles in newspapers and magazines. The latest edition to the garden is a fine brick and Norfolk cobble water feature, designed by Jim, with a cast phosphor bronze shell, sculptured by Gilbert Ward. In 2001 we agreed to open the garden for the National Gardens Scheme and had much pleasure in receiving visitors and raising money for NGS charities'

Jim and Jan Saunt's thronging visitors were no match for an invasion on 1 June 2009. In the early morning sun of that day 9000 "Frenchmen" arrived in Strumpshaw, completing a journey which began in the Loire Valley four weeks before. The host was Kevin London and his arrivals were day-old French Partridge chicks, hatched earlier that morning, at Ludham, from fertile eggs laid in France. Kevin is the modern counterpart of Strumpshaw's traditional gamekeeper, meeting the needs of a new generation of shooting sportsmen:

'French Partridges, in the natural state wouldn't lay

Above: *Mark Cox providing shelter for partridges in 2009.*

Left: *Kevin London, crating mature French Partridges in preparation for release.*

Kevin London, centre, counting the 'bag', October 2009.

William and friends. Left to right: Ross Beales, William Key, Darren Eadie, Matt Beales.

till June. We need them earlier to start shooting in September so they wouldn't be mature enough. We can't shoot a bird unless it's over 18 weeks, hence, the French have sown up this place in the Loire valley. They just lay brilliantly in there but they rely on the English market, completely. Hardly any are turned off in France, they all come here'

The 9000 chicks were put into houses, holding about 400 each. Dry litter of shredded cardboard covered the ground as any other product could be taken as food. Light, heat, water, specialist feed and twenty-four attention, seven days a week would bring them to maturity in ten weeks. The French variety are hardier than their English counterparts although there is a 2% allowance for the mortality rate.

Kevin tends his flock seven days a week assisted by Adam Hilburn, "who's a good chap." He relies on someone committed. There is no rest time with a field of pens; up and down, to and fro, watering, feeding in all weathers. A caravan is parked ready for the nights when 24 hour attention might be necessary. The field is an intensive care unit.

Once the day-olds had settled in to English life 4000 more shells were cracking open in Kevin's own incubator, the latest technology, made in France. This time it was pheasants, from eggs of local birds, caught at the end of the shooting season before being let go again. The eggs have spent 24 days of incubation.

Kevin London was born into gamekeeping when his family worked on the Woodbastwick Estate. He was destined to follow and spent four years there as an under-keeper then decided to travel to Australia and the Far East. On return, he worked on the Strumpshaw Hall estate and was eventually offered the shoot to rent by Jimmy Key. He built it from nine to more than forty days of shooting a year to the point where the sport is different to the past:

William Key, 2009.

'It used to be rich landowners inviting their rich friends but now it's accessible to everybody. But it's not cheap. For example, I've got a lorry driver who doesn't smoke, drink or play golf. He saves the money and is able to afford some nice days out in the winter-time. Others come from the building trade but it's slowed a bit now. I have to guarantee a good bag. If they pay for an amount of birds they expect them. We're not expensive, about the middle to the bottom.

It's affordable to local people, and I have a lot of local people'

After ten or twelve weeks the French Partridges are ready for the release but not straight into the wild. Spread about the estate are release-pens in specially planted cover strips of maize. The birds go into these refuges, fed and watered daily before, gradually, a few are let out. They tend not venture far or even escape because all their needs are at hand. But there are unwanted predators, foxes and birds of prey. There are 34 acres in total and local farmer, Peter Rant, comes in to sow the seeds of sunflowers and other fancy varieties, in these cover areas.

Tuesday 21 October 2009 was almost a typical shoot. It was another of those days which Kevin London had been anticipating for the past 18 weeks except the weather was dreadful. Soon after nine o'clock the 'guns' started to arrive and the beaters assembled around Adam Hilburn. Kevin, while anxious that enough birds would be flushed from their covers was out to enjoy this untypical day; he was a guest on the shoot of William Key, great-great-grandson of William J Holmes. Almost 130 years ago William's great-great-grandfather had bought the Strumpshaw estate.

Coffee and tea preceded the draw for gun positions. William's other guests were Matt & Ross Beales, farming associate Henry Alston, Richard Forder, Tom Laird and Darren Eadie, former Norwich City footballer. Shooting may be available to everyone but its following remains deep-rooted in tradition. Even the dress code united past and present.

Out in the fields there was driving rain and driven birds. The fully grown 'Fenchmen' took to the wing, urged and scared by flag-waving beaters. The guns proved true sportsmen taking birds at the highest altitude. A few pheasants plummeted, caught retreating from sodden woodland where dripping leaves sent them flying as retrieving dogs responded to whistling masters. The bag was around 200 by the end of the day. Kevin London may have been a guest but the game-loaded trailer bore the spoils of his twelve weeks nurturing.

In 2009 William Key was following a tough act. There were, and still are, those who would usurp the lineage of the squire but they must remember that presently, we live in a foreign country, where some things are not being done differently.

SUBSCRIBERS

Margaret and Gerald Adams

Martin Geofrey Adams and Stewart Graham Adams, Strumpshaw

Glenda M. Anderson, London

Kiki Angelrath (née Key), Strumpshaw

Annie and Rod, Shoulder of Mutton

Margaret (Peggy) Armond (née Bartram), Costessey

Sheila Ashford

Tony and Jo Atkins, Beighton, Norfolk

Tina Atkins, Norwich

Richard Atkins, Beighton, Norfolk

Thomas and Judith Atkins, Comberton, Cambs

Barbara and Peter Ayers, Brundall, Norfolk

Mr and Mrs L. Baker

Vincent Ball, Lingwood

Janice M. Bane, Strumpshaw, Norfolk

Cyril and Sherry Bardwell, Lingwood

Steve and Liz Barker, Strumpshaw

Mrs B. Barker née Edith Trett, née Easter, Brundall

Mrs Barrett, Strumpshaw

David Barrett, Lyng

Chris and Gillian (née Marriott) Bartram, Strumpshaw

Shirley Basey-Fisher, Strumpshaw, Norfolk

Keith and Rita Bedford, Strumpshaw, Norfolk

Jenny Blackburn and Ian Stones, Shoulder of Mutton, Strumpshaw, Norfolk

Christine Blowers, Lingwood, Norfolk

Marie and Roger Breame, Lingwood, Norfolk

Ted Brighton, Brundall

Barbara Brinded

C. Brooks, Lingwood, Norfolk

Graham and Doona Broom, Christchurch, New Zealand

Martin and Jennifer Broom, Strumpshaw

Emma Broom, Swannington, Norfolk

Raymond Broom and Madeline Broom (née Rose), Strumpshaw

Philip Buller, Sarratt, Hertfordshire

Marion and David Bullock, Thorpe End, Norfolk

Mrs Jennifer Burgess (née Payne),

Martha-Jane Burton and Glen Burton, Strumpshaw, Norfolk

The Cameron Family, Strumpshaw

Sarah Cartwright, Lackford End, Strumpshaw

Ken, Sandra and Darren Church

Sheila Cianchi

Dr F. R. Cianchi

Rob Cianchi

Chris Cianchi

David Cianchi

Peter Cianchi

Tim Cianchi

Monica A. Corthine, Strumpshaw

Joe and Beryl Cullum, Buckenham

Janet A. A. Cunningham, Strumpshaw

Terry and Anthea Dabbs

Alf Downs, Gorleston, Norfolk

Paul Downs, Canada

Christine Evans, Lingwood

David and Gloria Fagg, Strumpshaw

Duncan and Julie Foley, Strumpshaw

Geoffrey W. Forder, Strumpshaw

Raymond Forder, Rochdale, Lancs

Mary Forder, Strumpshaw, Norfolk

Iris and Derek Forster, Blofield, Norfolk

The Fox Family, Strumpshaw

Iris Gale, Strumpshaw

Michelle Garrod aka Chimelle, Swadeston, Norfolk

Jean George, Cantley

John and Mary Goward, Blofield Heath, Norfolk

Adrian Grand, Blofield, Norfolk

Sally J. Greenhill, Strumpshaw

Sheila J. Greenhill, Strumpshaw

Susan J. Greenhill, Strumpshaw

Mr and Mrs R. Guymer, Brundall

Dennis and Pam Harding

Gerry Hawkins, Brundall

Stephen Hearnden, Strumpshaw

Tony and Sue Hedge, Buckenham, Norfolk

Roger E. Hewitt, Hemsby

Charlotte Hovey, Strumpshaw

Nick and Mandy Hovey, Strumpshaw

Sarah Hovey, Strumpshaw

Olivia Hovey, Strumpshaw

Ernest and Coral Hoyos, Lingwood

Gloria J. Hurst, North Walsham, Norfolk

Helen James, Blofield, Norfolk

John Jenkins, Leeds

Ron and Maureen Jenkins, Strumpshaw

Anthony Clive Jermy, Herefordshire

Jo, Hoste, Laura and Sam

Heather Jones, Lingwood

The Kemp Family, Buckenham Road, Strumpshaw

Mrs Janet F. Kett, Strumpshaw, Norfolk

William James Holmes Key, Strumpshaw

Pauline and Don Kinmond, Buckenham

Elizabeth and Harry Knock, Gorleston, Norfolk

Paul and Sue Leech

The London Family, Strumpshaw

David Lynn, Lingwood, Norfolk

Wendy and Duncan Lyon, Niagara Falls, Canada

Joseph C. Mallett, Strumpshaw, Norfolk

George and Muriel Mallett, Strumpshaw

Arthur and Rita Marriott, Strumpshaw

Doris Mayes, Blofield, Norfolk

Christine McNamara, Strumpshaw, Norfolk

Colin and Celia Miller

Alistair Milner, Kegworth, Derby

Bertie and Myra Moore, Lingwood

Irene Negus and Roy Foster,

Bryan Nicholls, Thorpe St Andrew

Steven L. Oakley, Birmingham, West Midlands

Edie Ogden, Strumpshaw, Norfolk

Craige Olley and Beverley Ling, Strumpshaw, Norfolk

Lily Patterson, Wandsworth, London

Oscar Patterson, Wandsworth, London

Ben and Celia (née Peart) Patterson, Wandsworth, London

Felix Patterson, Wandsworth, London

Tony Patterson

Margaret Patterson, Blofield, Norfolk

Tony Patterson, Lingwood

Graham and Emma Patterson, Brisbane, Australia

Mrs Anne Payne, Blofield, Norfolk

Mrs W. Payne, Blofield, Norfolk

Giles Peart, Strumpshaw

District Councellor Shirley Peters, Lingwood

David and Barbara Pilch, Blofield

The Pinder Family, Strumpshaw

Dorothy Pleshko (née Atkins), PA, USA

Michael and Joan Powlesland

Nick and Judy Price

Patricia Roberts, Strumpshaw

Elsie Roberts, Strumpshaw

Mrs H. Rose, Blofield

Glenn Rowland, Brundall, Norfolk

Mr and Mrs D. J. Rowland

Maureen Rowland

Juliet Sallis, Ormesby

Janette and James Saunt, Strumpshaw, Norfolk

Jane Seaman, Reading, Berkshire

Ann and Keith Seaman, Reading, Berkshire

Carroll Sewell (née Piggin), fomerly of Strumpshaw

David Shiret, Strumpshaw, Norfolk

Jayne Short (née Walpole), Lingwood

William Simmons, Strumpshaw, Norfolk

Connie Squires, Bicester, Oxford

Mark S. Stone

Susan Stone, Lingwood, Norfolk

John Thomson, Brundall

Janet Todman, Blofield, Norfolk

Gray Tony

Keith and Brenda Tubby (née Trice), Acle

Michael Turner, Strumpshaw, Norfolk

Sue Turner, Lingwood, Norfolk

Mags Voke, Malvern, Victoria, Australia

The Revd David Wakefield, Lingwood

Lewis and Betty Warman, Strumpshaw, Norfolk

Simon P. Wicks

Kenny Wilkins, Strumpshaw

Ian Williams, formerly of Strumpshaw School

Ethel Wright, Lingwood

Richard and Pat Yallop